THE WORLD OF
RACING CARS

THE WORLD OF
RACING CARS

ERIC DYMOCK

Hamlyn
London New York Sydney Toronto

Published by The Hamlyn Publishing Group Limited
London, New York, Sydney, Toronto
Hamlyn House, Feltham, Middlesex, England
Copyright © The Hamlyn Publishing Group Limited 1972

ISBN 0 600 39240 6

Printed in Spain by Mateu-Cromo, Pinto, Madrid

Contents

Introduction by Jackie Stewart 6
The First Seventy Years 7
The Racing Car Evolves 30
Great Names in Racing 40
Ladder to the Top 57
Great Drivers 62
World Championship 86
Corners 94
Sports Car Racing 104
The Million Dollar Motor Races 111
The World Wide Scene 117
Index 127

Introduction by Jackie Stewart

One of the first people ever to watch me drive a racing car of any sort was Eric Dymock. He has been associated with my career ever since, which means he has seen a lot of tracks, met a lot of people, and watched a lot of races.

He has accumulated a wide knowledge of motor racing in all its different aspects. To this he has added his great writing ability to produce a book which is not only authoritative and interesting, but covers some of the most exciting years in the growth of the sport. The World Championship series of races alone has grown in breadth and prestige enormously, while more people are watching more motor races than ever before, and reading about it in the pages of the daily newspapers, and the motoring press. Eric's book sets out to portray motor racing, show its scope, and cover its international aspect. It is now an accepted activity in almost every part of the world.

One of motor racing's greatest attractions is its colour. This book has used magnificent colour printing to great advantage, bringing out the glamour of races as seen through the lenses of some of the best photographers in the business.

Eric Dymock takes a look at the past; motor racing is not an entirely new sport, although it has changed a great deal. Sometimes I feel he looks back with envy at what happened in years gone by. He has looked at the great names, their great cars, and the great races, and also at the ways that are open for new drivers to come up in the sport–the great names of the future perhaps.

The World of Racing Cars is a good read from one of the best informed writers on motor racing I know.

The First Seventy Years

The urge to compete has been with man since time began, and with centuries of horsemanship behind them it was hardly surprising that the early motorists parodied equestrianism with their cars. On the basis that anything *your* horse can do, mine can do better, and their new pride of ownership in cars, the motoring pioneers, who could only just make their horseless carriages go at all, began racing.

The first competitions were simple, private, unofficial and for the most part unrecorded duels between friends, anxious perhaps to prove petrol against steam, or steam against electrics. These were perhaps matters of seeing if the top of a hill could be reached, or how far a car could be driven without breaking down. Soon the object was to see how quickly the hill could be climbed or how fast a car would travel. Motor sport was born.

Little imagination is needed to see the motives behind simple trials of speed, but it is perhaps harder to grasp why great companies have spent lavishly on motor sport. However, it seems that as a technical exercise, a sport, a branch of show business or an advertising medium – however you like to regard it – motor sport, and especially racing, has a compelling attraction. It is intriguing to think beyond the recorded facts of racing history, to the reasons why people and companies have supported it. . . .

Those straightforward early duels evolved logically, and out of them came the series of officially timed runs which were to pass into history as the first speed records for cars (trains had been faster for years).

In 1898 the Comte Gaston de Chasseloup-Laubat covered a kilometre at a speed of 39.24 mph, in the Parc Agricole at Achères, just north of Paris. A little earlier in the year the Belgian driver Camille Jenatzy had won the Chanteloup hill-climb at 16 mph, and the two met at the Parc Agricole. Here Jenatzy failed to complete his run, but in the gentlemanly manner of the period challenged the comte to a return match, and this was extended to a series of encounters. In April 1899 Jenatzy covered the kilometre in 34 seconds in his electric car 'La Jamais Contente', thus becoming the first motorist to exceed 100 kilometres per hour – his actual speed was 65.79 mph.

In 1904 a speed of 100 mph was officially recorded for the first time, when Louis Rigolly achieved 103.56 mph at Ostend. By this time racing had passed through its first phase, and in 1903 Jenatzy's 1899 speed had almost been matched as the *average* between Paris and Bordeaux. . . .

The first actual race was run in 1895, barely ten years after Karl Benz had driven his first car on the road, and was a marathon test for primitive machinery from Paris to Bordeaux and back. Twenty-two vehicles set out, 15 powered by petrol engines, 6 by steam and 1 by electricity (this fell out in the early stages). The winner, Emile Levassor drove a twin-cylinder Panhard, and covered the 732 miles at 15 mph.

This event set the pattern for the short age of town to town races. Most of these were run in France, which was the leading nation in the early days of racing. It had a government which was sympathetic to motoring, and usually to racing; it had a thriving motor industry; its roads were open, long, and straight. A gallic spirit of competition made France the spiritual home of motor racing, and French was to be its language for many years to come.

In all there were some 35 town to town races. Speeds rose alarmingly and in winning the 1900 837-mile Paris-Toulouse-Paris race Levegh averaged 40.2 mph. Trouble came with the first accidents, notably in the 1901 Paris-Berlin when Richard Brasier killed a boy who was standing in the middle of the road. This provoked M Waldeck Rousseau, Minister of the Interior, to state that racing would be banned.

Chicago, 1895, the first race in America. The event was organized by the Chicago *Times Herald* and the course shortened because of snow. This twin-cylinder Duryea won.

Yet these races went on until 1903, when the zenith was reached in what should have been the Paris-Madrid race, but in fact became the Paris-Bordeaux race. A very large field of 275 vehicles, 112 of them the very fast but often flimsy 'heavy cars', set off and, wrote Charles Jarrott, who placed a de Dietrich fourth, '...disorder reigned supreme'. The carnage on what was intended to be the first stage was terrible–there was more than a dozen serious accidents as cars raced through clouds of dust, past spectators who had little conception of the speeds at which they were travelling. This drove home the lesson that motor racing was dangerous, if it was to be allowed at all, it must take place on closed circuits (which were already coming into use).

A contemporary wrote of one of the accidents: 'The most terrible sight of all was the wreck of Lorraine Barrow's car. It was the most complete wreck ever known. When doing over 80 mph he struck a dog. A child dashed out and a soldier rushed to save it. The body of the dog had jammed the steering, with the result that both soldier and child were run down and killed and the car went end-on into a tree. One of the front dumb irons was driven up to the hilt into the tree. The leather strap holding the starting handle cut its way into the solid wood. The motor was wrenched out of the frame and hurled yards away with the flywheel and crankshaft torn out of the engine. Even the pistons came adrift and were found nearly twenty yards further on. The frame, gearbox and road wheels were in fragments scattered around the grass verge'.

According to Jarrott, Bordeaux was filled that night with an anxious, terrified crowd. Most of the drivers were shaken by the experience, and there was talk of abandoning the event. Mors driver Fernand Gabriel led at Bordeaux, having covered the 342 miles from Paris at the staggering speed of 65.3 mph. Louis Renault, whose family gave their

Paris-Madrid, 1903 (above). Charles Jarrott, pioneer British driver who renounced a career in law to go motor racing, arriving at Bordeaux. Below: the Chevalier René de Knyff waiting to start his Panhard in the 1902 Paris-Vienna race

name to the Renault car had actually finished the stage first; he left Bordeaux that night to go to his brother Marcel, dying after an accident.

'The French government decided the matter for everybody concerned. The race was stopped forthwith, and all the racing cars taken possession of by the authorities. Special trains were secured, and the cars were dragged to the railway station behind horses and returned to Paris; not even the motors were allowed to start.'

Despite the end of town to town racing, and the growth of circuit races which could be policed better, the primary reason for the whole thing remained largely the sale of cars. Racing was already more than a sport; races were competitive public demonstration runs, tests to destruction carried out long before Consumerism had been invented. The philosophy of selling cars through racing in one form or another was to persist.

In 1902 the industry in France already employed 180,000 people, and made around 1,000 cars a month. It exported goods worth a million pounds a year, and the domestic tyre industry (largely Michelin) had a turnover of three quarters of a million pounds.

This industry soon became frustrated with the Gordon Bennett series of international team contests, which were the most important events once town to town racing was banned. To the French it appeared unjust that they should be restricted to three entries, no more than countries such as Britain, which had only small motor industries. So the Grand Prix was devised, open to teams from any number of manufacturers, irrespective of country: Brasier, Clément-Bayard, De Dietrich, Darracq, FIAT, Gobron-Brillié, Gregoire, Hotchkiss, Itala, Mercedes, Panhard and Renault took part in the 1906 French Grand Prix.

With the establishment of circuits, and the decay of the Gordon Bennett series of races, the Grand Prix was formalised with a series of regulations that came eventually to apply to several races. Initially, rules were drawn up for one event, but the idea of class regulations, later to become known as the Formulae, was growing. These were, and are, in effect sets of rules, guaranteed by the international ruling body to last for periods of time, with which

Above: a Renault during the last Gordon Bennett race, in 1905. Disputes led to this series being replaced by Grands Prix.
Opposite, top: David Bruce-Brown refuelling his Fiat in the 1912 French Grand Prix; he led at three-quarter distance, but was disqualified. This outstanding young American driver was killed later in the year.
Opposite, lower: Felice Nazzaro cornering an Itala in a cloud of dust and smoke in the 1913 French Grand Prix

racing cars for the principal international events would comply.

Competitors still paid to enter races. Manufacturers still had to build special cars, and although closed circuits had been introduced there was very little contribution paid by spectators. In terms of modern money, it has been estimated that the French Grand Prix at Le Mans in 1906 cost the equivalent of nearly a million pounds sterling to put on. It cost the organisers £60,000, and for each of the eleven teams it represented an investment of up to £75,000. Motor racing has not become a great deal more expensive in relative terms over the years, but the investment gradually came to be spread out over an entire season.

The massed start was still in the future. Starting competitors singly, or in pairs at minute intervals, was a legacy from town to town racing. Spectators' interests hardly counted at all, and the circuits were

Indianapolis, 1913. One of the European challengers, Georges Boillot (Peugeot)

so long that the cars were seen perhaps once an hour. It must have been all but impossible to follow the course of a race, even though with the inception of the closed circuit the same officials started and finished it. As in the old town to town events, it cannot have been easy to determine who was ahead of whom until the times were in, and all the sums done.

The cars before the First World War were controlled by regulations under which they gradually evolved from the spidery horseless carriage, to something approaching the classic racing car, with two seats and open wheels.

In 1906 the rules specified a maximum weight of 1,000 Kg (2,204 lbs) on rather empirical grounds. Cars still seemed sporting instruments, probably looked upon rather like yachts, to be measured in length, or tonnage. Hopefully it was felt that common sense would prevail, and designers would curb power and outright speed to ensure that cars would corner well, but the arithmetic of automotive design is not like that. Without restrictions, designers simply made their engines bigger and bigger to get more and more power, as they had for years.

So, for 1907 a fuel consumption Formula was decided upon, of 30 litres per 100 kilometres

(9.4 mpg). But even that did not stimulate design very much, which was certainly one of the organisers' aims, so for 1908 the authorities were a little more subtle. Piston area was limited to 117 square inches, and a *minimum* weight was applied of 1,150 Kg (2,534 lbs). In 1912 fuel was limited again, this time to 20 litres per 100 kilometres (14.2 mpg) and minimum weight reduced to 800 Kg (1.760 lbs) and a maximum weight reintroduced at 1,100 Kg (2,425 lbs).

This 1912 French Grand Prix marked a turning point in racing history. Whereas the previous major Grands Prix, the 1908 French and American races, had been won by a 13.5 litre Mercedes and a 12 litre Fiat respectively, at Dieppe in 1912 Georges Boillot drove a 7.6 litre Peugeot to victory (at 68.45 mph over 956 miles—there were no half-measures about making that race a demanding test of stamina!). The Mercedes and the Fiat had been traditional cumbersome machines, with large-capacity slow-running engines driving through chains, but the Peugeot had a relatively high-revving four-valve twin overhead camshaft engine, driving through a propeller shaft.

In running the Grand Prize of the Automobile Club of America, that country became the second to stage a Grand Prix (the first international race run in the USA was the Vanderbilt Cup on a Long Island circuit in 1904). For a few years, the Grand Prize was the pre-eminent American race, until it was displaced by the Indianapolis 500.

Not until 1914 was engine capacity selected as a convenient means of giving all racing cars equivalent opportunities. This $4\frac{1}{2}$ litre limit provided designers with a framework in which to lay down new cars, and had the virtue of being an easy rule to enforce, needing no more than an elementary measuring device.

In the years before 1906, the leading makers used engines of 11 to 16 litres, with power outputs between 90 and 120 bhp. These engines were rather ponderous affairs, doing about 1,200 rpm and driving the rear wheels through chains (still used by five entrants for the first Grand Prix). Wooden chassis had practically given way to steel; bodies were flimsy. The large tyres were prone to punctures, and the wheels carried mostly on beam axles with semi-elliptic springs. However, the pioneers were nothing if not innovators. Many of them introduced features which proved to be years ahead of their time, but often they lacked the technology or the materials, or the manufacturing skills to make their best ideas work. In 1903, for example, the 8 cylinder engine appeared, and a supercharged Chadwick was raced in America in 1908. Independent front suspension, inclined overhead valves, and overhead camshaft engines were all seen in racing, while Mors cars with the earliest forms of shock absorber had been raced in 1899. Towards the end of the Edwardian era, cars were smaller, with more efficient high-speed engines running at 3,000 rpm, and four wheel brakes were introduced.

By 1914, one lap of the French Grand Prix circuit at Lyons was 'only' 23.3 miles, and the winner's speed for the 468-mile race was 65.3 mph, despite the comparatively restricting nature of the regulations.

The emphasis in racing was still on the sales battle. Companies raced to sell cars, and amongst the incentives was the development that racing encouraged. Test tracks, and associated development procedures lay in the future. What better way for an engineer to measure the performance of his creation than to race it against his competitors? Racing was more than a sport; it was the motor industry's research tool, as well as its shop window. It was a prestige affair for the companies, although as the war clouds gathered in 1914, nationalism began to play a part.

People were taking sides, not with the makes of cars as before, but with the countries building them.

Motor racing in 1914 reflected the mood of the age, as it was to do again twenty years later.

In July 1914, Archduke Ferdinand had met the assassin's bullet at Sarajevo, and all over Europe trigger fingers were itchy. With representatives of most of the likely contesting countries in the war they must have known was imminent, the crowd at Lyon, watching the last Grand Prix of the era, had a polite foretaste of the horror that was to follow.

For motor racing in the grand manner, the 1920s can be counted in some ways as a period of decline, for with the emphasis shifting to mass production, racing came to matter less to the big firms. They could hardly hope to encourage customers for popular Tens, Eights or Sevens with lightweight high-performance two-seaters, even though a change in the Formula brought engine capacity down from 3 litres in 1921 to 2 litres. It was further reduced in 1926 to $1\frac{1}{2}$ litres and although from then on the hitherto obligatory riding mechanic was banished (the job had never been a sinecure, now it was downright dangerous) the cars remained for the time being two seaters. A major technical development was the adoption of supercharged engines, which by and large were to reign supreme until 1950.

Between the wars America completely lost interest in 'European-style' road racing, somewhat ironically as in 1921 Jimmy Murphy won the French Grand Prix with a Duesenberg, which to this day remains the only Grand Prix victory for a wholly American car. In Europe, however, Grand Prix racing spread beyond France, with the first Italian Grand Prix run in 1921, and the first Belgian, German, British, Spanish, and Monaco events later in the decade.

Factory support continued through the first half of the decade, but with a difference, for of the major firms only Fiat ran a Grand Prix team. Small specialist firms filled the gap, at least until the late 1920s when for a while the field was left almost entirely to private owners.

Alfa Romeo, for example, was a small firm concentrating on sporting cars, and thus had reason enough to race. So had Ettore Bugatti, who personified the breed of engineer that motor racing was to throw up again and again through the years; an engineer with the mechanical equivalent of green fingers. A man who would make cars, not merely because he knew his algebra and could look up stress tables, but because he had a sense of engineering style.

Plainly, the incentives that had lain behind racing in the Edwardian era no longer existed. It was symptomatic of this that instead of teams paying entry fees for the privilege of racing, organisers had to be prepared to pay for them coming. Oil and tyre

companies began backing private teams as the support from the car makers dwindled and then vanished altogether. The oil and tyre people recognised the advertising opportunities, because racing had become established as a popular spectacle. It was something the family went to watch in their new Sevens, Eights and Tens. Even if they only saw it on Southport Sands.

Inevitably, the attention of the new enthusiasts focused on drivers. It was an era in international racing of characters who caught the imagination, and racing drivers were popular heroes. But there was a development which in some ways put the clock back.

In the beginning, races had been competitions between cars built for the road; there were no cars of any other sort. Their employment for racing was incidental. Now, as racing cars became increasingly specialised, there was a reversion—some people broke away from the mainstream of Grands Prix, and again began to race cars that had been built simply as transport. Sports and touring car races were inaugurated and became the only racing that a sensible manufacturer could afford to be involved with—a sensible manufacturer like Bentley.

Once again, this new racing aimed partly at stimulating improvements in design. The 24-hour race at Le Mans spurred on improvements in

Above: first major American victory in European racing. Jimmy Murphy and his mechanic Ernie Olsen winning the 1921 French GP for Duesenberg.
Opposite, top: Ernst Friedrich in the T30 'Tank' Bugatti during the 1923 French GP. The rounded nose was to find an echo nearly fifty years later.
Opposite, lower: One of the most successful racing cars ever, the Bugatti Type 35 in its debut race, the 1924 French GP.
Below: Another early streamliner, the Benz Tropfenrennwagen of 1923

lighting, and in another practical aspect, for in the second race in 1924 all the competitors were obliged to stop, erect their cars' hoods and complete two laps with them up. Restrictions on the amounts of fuel, oil, and water which could be taken on also aimed to help development. As 'Le Mans' was established as a spectacle, a week-end *en fête*, a new dimension in motor racing became apparent. As well as a test bench, sales window, and sport, it was becoming more and more an entertainment.

Yet during the 1920s racing remained a sport more than anything else. This was the principal reason why wealthy amateurs pitted their skill against great Continental professionals like Varzi and Nuvolari (although professional/amateur distinction was not applied as in some other sports). These were the years of the Bugatti, with their severe lines, pointed tails and horseshoe radiators, which came to characterize the classic shape of the Grand Prix car. It was still nominally a two seater, and it was now more obviously an open wheeler, because sports cars had recognisable bodywork, mudguards, and headlamps. The Grand Prix car was lean, low, and athletic, an impression to be reinforced early in the 1930s when true single-seaters appeared.

The giants. Pit stop for Rudi Hasse Auto Union in the 1936 German Grand Prix (above). The mechanics refuel, change the rear wheels (note the mechanic hammering off an eared wheel fixing) and offer the driver a drink. Hasse finished the race in fourth place.
Left: Manfred von Brauchtisch leading his team mate Rudi Caracciola through the Station Hairpin at Monaco, towards a Mercedes 1-2-3 at Monaco in 1937

Despite the amateurism, and the lack of works support, Grand Prix racing survived into the 1930s. New drivers appeared, like Rudi Caracciola, the former mechanic who drove for Mercedes-Benz, Louis Chiron, the Monegasque with his matinee idol looks and his blue Bugattis. Alfa Romeo and Maserati fought it out with Bugatti in races like the Targa Florio, the dusty Sicilian event which was to survive into the 1970s as a race for sports cars. There were world championships of sorts, which received little attention, but Grand Prix racing was spreading.

Other races were as important, but were called something else, like the Coppa Ciano, run at Montenero, or the Coppa Acerbo, at Pescara. Monza, Monaco, Nürburgring, Spa and Montlhéry were amongst the circuits that came into use in the 1920s, and were to survive in much the same shape for the next four decades and more. With them the

pattern of motor racing, and its fragmentation into different categories, was established.

Now, a new influence came to bear. The era of European dictatorships arrived, and Italy and Germany sought every means to establish and demonstrate technical superiority. They fastened on motor racing as a modern Twentieth Century, mechanised (to use a word they were fond of then) chariot race, where they could show the world that *their* engineering was better than that of anyone else.

As a sport, pure and simple, motor racing at the highest levels was finished. It no longer had a sales influence, except marginally in the sports or touring area. The chosen instruments of the Nazis, Mercedes-Benz and Auto-Union, and the Italian Fascists, Alfa Romeo, were comfortably subsidised, so commercial justifications for racing no longer applied. Nor was it any longer such a field for development. This was done *before* cars appeared on the circuit because failure was unthinkable. It was the Space Race of the Thirties.

The amateurs were laughed off the tracks. Other manufacturers quit because being beaten so thoroughly (as they were by the Germans) did nothing at all for sales or anything else. There was no doubt about the triumph of the new order.

17

The formula which came into force in 1934, and was to last for four years, governed weight to 750 Kg (1,653 lbs or 14.73 cwt), and imposed minimum body width of 85 cm (33½ in) but did not restrict engine capacity. This omission led to some astonishing cars.

The winter of 1933 saw Alfa Romeo preparing new 2.9 litre versions of the hitherto successful P3 model for Scuderia Ferrari, the team which which represented them in racing. This car had seldom been beaten in its two seasons of racing and therefore appeared to set the standard for the new formula. Maserati also had a 2.9 litre eight cylinder engine, and Bugatti a new 2.8 litre. This type 59 was a strikingly well proportioned successor to the outstanding Bugatti type 35. These three cars were logical developments of existing models, and thus appeared promising.

However, the Germans were getting ready for the most determined onslaught on Grand Prix racing yet. Hitler's government had offered £40,000 for the most successful German car of 1934. Mercedes, now Mercedes-Benz, returned to racing after a lapse of ten years, and Auto-Union, a recently formed consortium, took up a design by Dr Ferdinand Porsche. The former produced a workmanlike 3.3 litre eight

cylinder car with independent suspension to all four wheels. The Auto-Union was a highly unorthodox mid-engined sixteen cylinder car. Both were built virtually regardless of expense.

After a couple of false starts, the new cars with their superior power, backed up with good organisations and generous budgets, swept the board. They won between them all the races in the second half of the 1934 season, and only Alfa Romeo showed much of a challenge, although Bugatti briefly promised to stage a comeback.

The 1934 season set the pattern. Racing no longer depended on prize money or trade support, or sporting enthusiasm for its survival. It was propped up by two wealthy governments.

From 1935 to 1937, while the 750 Kg Formula remained in force, Mercedes-Benz and Auto-Union held the stage. Alfa Romeo's interjections became less frequent, and they owed much of what success

18

Grand Prix cars return to America (above). Bernd Rosemeyer, the great Auto Union driver, leading Caracciola's Mercedes in the 1937 Vanderbilt Trophy. Rosemeyer won, from Richard Seaman in a Mercedes.
Opposite: First racing car to have disc brakes, the disappointing rear-engined Gulf-Miller, built in 1938 by Harry Miller for the Indianapolis 500

they did have to the genius of one of their drivers, the redoubtable Mantuan, Tazio Nuvolari. From 1935 even this challenge was virtually eclipsed by the mighty German teams, now equipped with massive staffs of 300 people, and annual budgets around £250,000. Leading drivers were Caracciola for Mercedes-Benz, and Bernd Rosemeyer, who came to terms with the big Auto-Unions which although prophetic in their mid-engined layout, were notoriously difficult to handle. The science of road holding was not yet equal to Dr Porsche's impeccable logic in putting the engine in the middle of the car.

Engines had reached new heights of efficiency; it was this sort of engineering at which the Germans, with their great resources of design and drawing office talent, excelled. By 1937 the Auto-Union V-16 measured 6 litres, and with supercharging produced 520 bhp at 5,000 rpm. The contemporary Mercedes-Benz W125 was the most powerful Grand Prix car ever built, with a 5.6 litre straight-eight engine producing over 640 bhp. These two cars completely dominated the 1937 season, Auto-Union winning five races, Mercedes-Benz seven.

In an effort to counter this domination, the international regulations for 1938 and 1939 were amended to provide a relationship between weight and engine capacity, which was to be limited in any case to 3 litres with a supercharger, and

4½ litres without. The new cars were smaller, lighter and better streamlined, and in lap speeds they were even faster than the 1937 cars.

The change had little effect on the superiority of the German teams, which both chose the 3-litre supercharged alternative offered by the regulations. Auto-Union lost Rosemeyer when he died in a record-breaking attempt on the Frankfurt-Darmstadt autobahn, but almost at once took on Nuvolari, who despaired of finding a competitive Italian car.

So, at the outbreak of war, the Germans still held sway in Grands Prix. The futility of competing with them had one important result however; it encouraged other classes of racing. The 1½ litre class known by the French term 'Voiturette' since before the First World War, gained enormously in stature, especially as the leading Italian teams concentrated on it, rather than on futile attempts to match the German 3-litre cars.

Sports car racing had also blossomed, but as yet there were still no real world championships. Grand Prix was the 'blue-chip', premium racing, and although by no stretch of the class-warfare imagination of the 1930s would you ever define sports car racing as inferior; a later age might have referred to it euphemistically as slightly down-market.

Here, the contest was still between the different makes of car, and part of the incentive was sales. Drivers, even though they had caught the public imagination, like the 'Bentley Boys' at the end of the 1920s, were still not much more than unusually heroic chauffeurs. Racing still could not provide many of them with a living – most drivers paid for the privilege.

The pattern of each country having its annual Grand Prix had become established, although there was as yet no formal seasonal arrangement.

In America, the concentration was on track racing, from dirt tracks all over the country to the 2½ mile brick-surfaced oval at Indianapolis. Since 1911 this had been the venue of a race that had become a classic, the 500 Mile Motor Sweepstakes. In form and regulations the resemblance to Grand Prix was superficial, but pioneered features that were later to be adopted all over the world.

Although crowds of over 300,000 attended pre-war German Grands Prix, in 1939 motor racing as an entertainment had still not quite arrived in Europe, although the portents were there for anyone who would look. Perhaps the most important thing was that alternative forms of competition to Grands Prix had established themselves. Above all, it became possible to have motor racing that was *not* Grand Prix racing, without it looking like a poor relation. Touring cars, voiturettes, and sports cars of all denominations raced happily, sometimes together. But the Grands Prix had the status, the tradition, the sense of occasion – even the class – for a world championship.

It soon became clear that post-war racing would need to use pre-war cars, and racing was revived around these in free formula conditions. In 1948, however a new Grand Prix formula came into force, for single-seaters with engines of 1½ litres supercharged or 4½ litres unsupercharged. It thus admitted the pre-war supercharged voiturettes on the one hand, and the Delage and Talbot 4½ litre cars of the 1938–40 Grand Prix Formula on the other, and was to prove a well-balanced arrangement.

No supercharged 3 litre cars to speak of had survived the war. Most of the German factories were in ruins, and their cars were scattered; in any

Michael Turner

event, the Germans were not invited to join in racing. So far as the Grands Prix were concerned, they were non-starters. Equally the Italians had largely left the field in ignominy in 1939. But there were 1½ litre Alfa Romeos, ERAs and Maseratis, to make up fields with the 4½ litre French cars.

Of these existing cars, the Alfa Romeo 158, which in voiturette form had been known as the Alfetta, was the most advanced. It had an eight cylinder supercharged engine and was the only car to appear throughout the years of the new formula with independent suspension all round. For five years it was to be virtually unbeatable.

It seemed that its challenger would be the BRM, a most complex car with a supercharged 16 cylinder engine running at 12,000 rpm, which would have

been fast for a piston engine twenty years later. This design was laid down by the team which put the pre-war ERA together, although in part it was based quite cheerfully on a Daimler-Benz scheme for a 1940 car, a competitor for the Alfetta, which was never built owing to the war.

The BRM project was undertaken by a group financed by industry. It was based on the pre-war idea of prestige flowing from supremacy in motor racing to the benefit, it was supposed, of British industry as a whole. The BRM was to be a red carpet leading to the doors of export markets.

Alas, the idea was out of date. There was not enough money to support such an ambitious scheme, and in any case BRM never had the resources to develop such an advanced and complicated car.

Christian Lautenschlager winning the 1914 French Grand Prix at Lyon. A month before the outbreak of the First World War, the German cars finished first, second and third before a crowd of 300,000 people. Georges Boillot's ailing Peugeot, overtaken only two laps before the end of the race, follows the triumphant Mercedes

Times had changed; the carpet had been pulled from under BRM's feet. Motor racing, the prestige instrument of Nazi Germany, had reverted to a mongrel animal, part sport, part salesroom, part entertainment. Industry could not afford prestige at BRM's prices, and as yet there were not enough races on the calendar to pay for this sort of racing car.

The failure of the BRM was more than simply a tale of woe, of a gallant project that was unable to make its way in the world. It was a signal that the old order of motor racing was once again changing. It had been a spectacle, a laboratory, a shop front, and an expression of national pride. Now, more and more it was going to be an entertainment. For better or worse, it was never going to be the same again.

Above: Froilan Gonzalez (2 litre Maserati) at Silverstone in 1953.
Left , top: the first world champion, Giuseppe Farina, drifting an Alfa Romeo 159 in the 1951 British Grand Prix.
Opposite, below: Gonzalez at Silverstone again, in an historic race. The burly Argentinian drove this big Ferrari to defeat the highly-tuned 159 Alfas for the first time in the 1951 British Grand Prix

In the event the real challenge to Alfa Romeo came from Enzo Ferrari, who had set himself up as a manufacturer. The Italian teams had things pretty much their own way as the 1940s became the 1950s. The French challenged briefly with the Talbot, and the little Gordinis, but success lay where the support was. The Italians were well backed, the French were virtually running on private resources, and the British, in their innocence, pinned their faith in BRM, except for some brave amateurs with pre-war, upright and thoroughly out of date ERAs.

In 1951 the Alfas at last met their match. After attempting to challenge them on their own 1½ litre supercharged terms, Ferrari turned to a 12 cylinder unsupercharged 4½ litre engine which had an advantage in fuel consumption. This led to an arresting match, satisfying the need for technical interest, and proving the wisdom of the formula. Big Ferraris against smaller, slimmer highly tuned Alfa Romeos added drama to races, lent excitement to pit stops. In some ways it was a hang-over from pre-war days, and it was a high spot in motor racing. The idiom of the period was growth, and this battle had all the right elements. There were personalities – especially Ferrari versus Alfa Romeo for whom he had raced and run teams for so long and who had in part been responsible for the Alfetta. The great drivers of the immediate post-war era were all involved; Fangio, Ascari and Farina amongst them. The cars were the exciting, ear-splitting, high-revving supercharged Alfa eights and deep-throated Ferrari twelves. In an enthralling British Grand Prix, Gonzalez in a Ferrari beat the Alfas fairly and squarely, and during the rest of that season it became clear that the Alfa 158/159 had met its match. So Alfa Romeo retired from racing.

Their withdrawal left the field to Ferrari, and the faint promise of a BRM challenge. The Grand Prix formula therefore collapsed, and for two years the premier races were run to Formula 2 regulations for 2-litre unsupercharged cars. Under these, Maserati challenged Ferrari for race honours, then in 1954 new Grand Prix regulations came into force, permitting engines of 2½-litres, and the Italian teams faced the return of Mercedes-Benz.

The German company came back into Grand Prix racing with the W196, which dominated the Championship series, albeit through the genius of Fangio rather than the advanced mechanical make-up of the car. Its straight-eight engine was used in the essentially similar 300SLR sports car. One of these was involved in the 1955 Le Mans accident, in which over 80 people died, leaving the Mercedes-Benz racing plans in ruins, and reverberating through motor racing for years.

Some countries simply banned motor sport altogether. Circuits like Bremgarten, home of the Swiss Grand Prix were never used again. The memory of those eighty deaths, caused when Pierre Levegh's 300SLR flew amongst the crowd has haunted circuits ever since, and reinforced demands over the years to make motor racing safer.

By this time, the picture was changing, and the financial structure of the sport had altered out of all recognition. The wheel had turned full circle from the days when people paid to enter races. Now, they were demanding (and getting) £1,000 for each car at the start line. Prize money had lost its significance; it had remained at pre-war levels in many cases, and there was the faintly absurd situation of drivers racing £30,000 investments for a trifling purse of a few hundred pounds.

The oil and tyre companies were still the most prominent racing sponsors but they had sown the seeds of their own downfall. They supported teams largely by means of retainers, a method which was to get out of proportion. Bonus payments for wins alone still lay in the future.

In Grand Prix racing, the late 1950s saw the decline in Italian influence, and the arrival of the British with serious, competitive cars for the first time in thirty years. BRM it is true were still in the doldrums; Connaught and HWM struggling with inadequate budgets, but the Vanwall began winning races, and in 1958 took the Manufacturers' World Championship, with 48 points to Ferrari's 40. Third place also went to Britain, with a new car that was starting a revolution – the Cooper.

The drivers' world championship had been instituted in 1950 for Grand Prix racing, or Formula 1 as it became known owing to the fondness of the FIA, the international ruling body, for naming things with numbers.

This set the official seal upon the Grand Prix as the premier racing class; the world championship class, and so it was to remain.

Face to face at Rheims. Hans Herrman in the streamlined Mercedes-Benz W196, making a triumphant debut in the 1954 French Grand Prix, encounters Gonzalez spinning his Ferrari Type 553 Squalo. Right: British renaissance. Stirling Moss brings his Vanwall in at the end of the 1957 British Grand Prix at Aintree. He shared the car with Tony Brooks, to achieve the first championship Grand Prix victory for a British car

Other kinds of racing, particularly in North America could match it in money terms, there was even racing that was faster, or more exciting, or more interesting. Yet Formula 1 races, now mostly on traditional circuits, for open wheeled single seater racing cars, machines built with all the ingenuity of man for one purpose, came to be regarded as the summit in motor sport.

The pattern of each country holding its own Grand Prix, and awarding points in each race to decide the drivers' and manufacturers' championships was thus firmly established. Circuits varied from country to country, some preferring their traditional venues,

like Monaco, perhaps the most colourful of all tracks, round the streets of the Principality. Germany still had the Nürburgring, and Italy another traditional track in the Monza Park, near Milan.

Belgium continued to close the public roads in the Ardennes near Spa. France had a road course at Rheims, and a slightly twistier one at Rouen-les-Essarts. In Britain, Silverstone grew out of the wartime aerodrome, Brands Hatch was extended and Oulton Park built in answer to an explosive growth of interest. The Dutch built Zandvoort on the dunes near Haarlem. The demands of the different tracks were varied and important. They prevented racing cars, already in a sense automotive curiosities, from becoming complete freaks.

As motor racing had become an entertainment, and no matter how the traditionalists hated the idea, it lost even its justification as a development ground for production car ideas. 'The racing car of today is the touring car of tomorrow', was a phrase often bandied about in the motoring Press, but it was already out of date by 1939. Racing may have encouraged some technical developments (disc brakes are most often quoted, but in fact were developed for aircraft use). It is doubtful if racing had much influence on production cars after 1950, save on a few small-series sports cars.

While Grand Prix racing was established at the top of the tree, the branches grew more strongly. Voiturette racing had become Formula 2 in 1948, and there was a strong movement to bring racing within financial reach of more people, which led to the first Formula 3. This was for little motor cycle engined 500 cc single seaters, which in theory almost any enthusiast could build; in fact, the very professional series of Cooper cars soon became dominant in the class.

The 500 cc movement started in Britain, and for the most part remained there. Then the Italians launched Formula Junior, leading eventually to a new Formula 3, once again for single-seaters, this time with engines based on production car units. All of these third-level single seater formulae proved to be excellent 'cadet' classes, and in them drivers from Stirling Moss to Jackie Stewart first gained international recognition.

Meanwhile, a sports car championship for constructors had been introduced, and as sports car racing in the 1950s reached the rarified levels of the Grands Prix, so categories had to be introduced into this branch of the sport. Once again the impetus came from Britain, for British manufacturers built world-class sports cars before they were able to match Continentals in the Grand Prix class.

The 1950s also saw racing in the United States emerging from its isolationist shell, although track events remained the most important single type of racing – the Indianapolis 500 was a World Championship round until 1960. However, road racing spread rapidly, first at an amateur level, and largely concerned with sports cars. From this rediscovery came the transatlantic traffic familiar in the last decade, and during the 1960s world championship races became as firmly established in the New World as they were in Europe.

Each side had something to offer. The lure westwards lay mainly in the rich rewards for racing success in America; eastwards the prestige of at least trying to beat the long-established Europeans on their traditional circuits was a strong attraction, especially in the classic 24-hour race at Le Mans.

The Tasman series in New Zealand and Australia also began to attract top-class entries from Europe, while in 1961 the South African Grand Prix became a Formula 1 race contested by the European 'circus'.

As racing became a truly world wide sport, so it continued to change. Through these years, motor racing became more nearly driver racing, following a pattern well established in the United States. The drivers' world championship eclipsed all other championships in the minds of the general public, to the extent that many people became indifferent to the cars.

The public acclaimed Fangio, Moss, Clark or Stewart far more than Ferrari, Maserati, Mercedes-Benz, Matra or March. Graham Hill's serious accident in 1969 made more impact on the public mind than all the victories by all the cars in the entire season's racing. The cars had become chariots to everyone but the dyed-in-the-wool enthusiasts.

The era of the professional racing driver, entertainer and matador, had arrived.

Stirling Moss in his early days (top), driving a Cooper 500 the 'wrong' way up Paddock Bend in 1950, when races at Brands Hatch were run anticlockwise.
Britain's first world champion, Mike Hawthorn (below), driving a Cooper-Bristol at Goodwood in 1952. With this car, he shot to fame in the space of an afternoon by winning one race and finishing second to Gonzalez in another. By the end of the season, he had secured a works drive with Ferrari

The Racing Car Evolves

In the beginning there were just cars, pressed into service for racing. But very soon after the turn of the Century came the division, into cars that were used for racing, and those that were not. Then there were cars that *could* be used for racing but seldom were, and cars that were expressly built for the road but for which races were devised. Some racing cars could be used on the road and there were others that were useful racing machines once they had been suitably changed or modified. There were large areas of overlap.

Not until the 1920s did a definitive pattern really emerge. The table on page 33 is a guide to explain the evolution of different types of racing cars. The time-scale is notional, insofar as some of the developments actually happened before the date shown, but may not have become significant. 'Voiturettes', or light cars, for example were raced in categories of the early town-to-town events, and at least one voiturette circuit event, established in 1906, had gained considerable significance by 1912. But for most practical purposes, these secondary cars remained in the background until the mid-1930s. The distinction in the early years between cars built for racing, and road cars used for racing is necessarily blurred.

On the left of the table are cars built specifically for racing. The right begins with cars built principally for the road, but from its first major division around 1920, many of the cars on the sports side *were* built for racing; further down, in the 1950s, nearly all the two-seat sports/racing cars could hardly be used for anything *but* racing. By the time they are called two-seat racing cars, for that is just what they had become. Even on the touring car side, many cars were no more than racing machines manufactured from components resembling standard cars. Many never saw the inside of the factory whose name they bore. Generally, the left of the table contains the more radical *racing* cars, while those on the right remain closer to road cars.

The relationship between racing cars and road cars is an important one. The remoteness of racing from the cars people use every day has often been a source of contention. Through to the 1920s a degree of interchangeability persisted, but it gradually disappeared. The relevance to road cars became lost, even in many of the nominally touring car categories.

Cars that exemplify progress on the left are easy to find; those on the right less so. In Grands Prix, the first milestone is probably the car that hastened the demise of the pre-1910 monster racing cars. This 7.6 litre Peugeot came from the drawing board of Ernest Henry, a young Swiss engineer. It appeared in 1912, when Grand Prix racing resumed after a three year break, established a pattern that racing cars were to follow for the next twenty years, and pioneered features that were to remain *de rigeur* on racing cars for ever.

Henry's Peugeot introduced twin overhead camshafts, four valves per cylinder, and hemispherical combustion chambers, that found echoes decades later in Cosworth, Honda, Offenhauser, Ferrari, Porsche, and many other racing engines. The Peugeot won not only two Grand Prix races in 1912, but gained victory at Indianapolis the following year as well. Yet it was not so much its race successes that mark it out for distinction, as its influence, and that of the models derived from it between 1912 and 1914, on design in the years on either side of the First World War.

Peugeot's principal rival while the war-clouds were gathering over Europe in 1914 was the $4\frac{1}{2}$ litre

Upright cars of the early 1930s. Top: a 1934 T59 Bugatti. Its 3.3 litre supercharged straight-eight engine gave 240 bhp, and it was no match for German Grand Prix cars with twice the power.
Below: an Alfa Romeo P3, in the colours of Scuderia Ferrari, for whom Nuvolari drove great races in similar cars

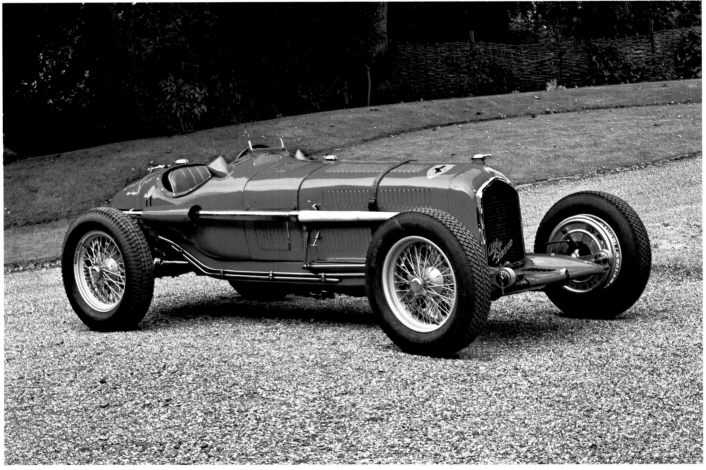

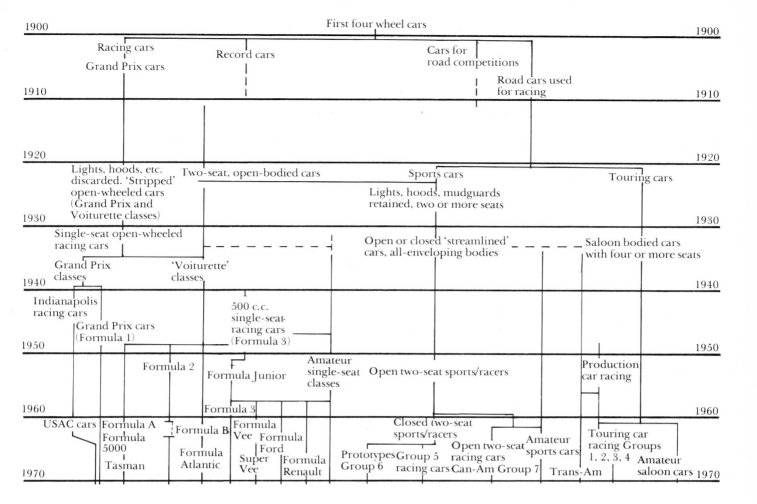

| 1900 | First four wheel cars | 1900 |

Racing cars
Grand Prix cars — Record cars — Cars for road competitions — Road cars used for racing

1910 ... 1910

1920 ... 1920

Lights, hoods, etc. discarded. 'Stripped' open-wheeled cars (Grand Prix and Voiturette classes) — Two-seat, open-bodied cars — Sports cars — Touring cars

Lights, hoods, mudguards retained, two or more seats

1930 ... 1930

Single-seat open-wheeled racing cars — Open or closed 'streamlined' cars, all-enveloping bodies — Saloon bodied cars with four or more seats

Grand Prix classes — 'Voiturette' classes

1940 ... 1940

Indianapolis racing cars
Grand Prix cars (Formula 1) — 500 c.c. single-seat racing cars (Formula 3)

1950 ... 1950

Formula 2 — Formula Junior — Amateur single-seat classes — Open two-seat sports/racers — Production car racing

1960 ... 1960

USAC cars | Formula A Formula 5000 Tasman | Formula B Formula Atlantic | Formula Vee Super Vee | Formula Ford Formula Renault | Closed two-seat sports/racers Prototypes Group 6 / Group 5 racing cars | Open two-seat racing cars Can-Am Group 7 | Amateur sports cars Trans-Am | Touring car racing Groups 1, 2, 3, 4 Amateur saloon cars

1970 ... 1970

Mercedes. Paul Daimler, its designer, followed the general pattern set by Henry, with a relatively small, four cylinder engine which had four valves per cylinder, but only one overhead camshaft. The dimensions of the engine complied with the 1914 Grand Prix Formula, and in the Grand Prix de l'Automobile Club de France, the event for which it was specifically designed, the Mercedes team gained the first three places, led by Christian Lautenschlager. During the war, the two makes continued their rivalry in the United States,. but the only time one of the German cars repeated the Lyons victory over the Peugeots was at Indianapolis in 1915, when the driver was Ralph de Palma.

The Mercedes remained competitive even after the war, winning the 1922 Targa Florio, and later formed the basis for a series of Mercedes sports car. It was one of the models responsible for the line at this period, linking the two sides of the table.

The origins of the next milestone are confused.

Top: Masetti winning the 1922 Targa Florio for Mercedes on the Madonie circuit in Sicily.
Below: Straight-eights in the 1921 French Grand Prix. Boyer (Duesenberg) on the left, and Goux (Ballot) on the finishing straight at Le Mans. Boyer retired while in second place, and Goux finished third

The straight-eight—or rather two *successful* straight-eights—appeared in both America and Europe soon after the First World War. Both engines owed more than inspiration to an eight-cylinder aircraft engine which Bugatti had designed during the war, for production in France by Baras (where Ernest Henry was works manager) and by Duesenberg in the USA. When Ballot commissioned Henry to design a car for the 1919 Indianapolis race, he came up with a d.o.h.c., four valve per cylinder eight; that same race saw a Duesenberg eight start. None of these cars performed conspicuously well in 1919, one of the Ballots finishing fourth.

Both makes returned with straight-eights in 1920, under the 183 cu in Indianapolis regulations, which coincided with the 3-litre European limit when Grand Prix racing resumed in 1921. In that year, Duesenberg won the French Grand Prix, Ballot the Italian Grand Prix, and the straight eight was established as the most favoured type of racing engine, a state of affairs which with occasional interruptions lasted into the 1950s. Curiously, neither Ballot nor Duesenberg featured again in Grand Prix racing, but the American company was prominent at Indianapolis through the 1920s, fielding the winning car in 1922, 1924, 1925 and 1927.

Ettore Bugatti developed his own racing version of his straight-eight for one of the most famous racing cars of all time, the Type 35 Bugatti. This was one of the first catalogued racing cars ever, and was built with a precision and craftsmanship which through the years have become legendary. Between 1924 and 1931 its cornering abilities gave it the edge on many more powerful cars, and won it innumerable races, including five consecutive Targa Florios (1925–29) and the Grands Prix of France, Belgium, Italy, Monaco and Spain, some of them twice (although it must be admitted that it was seldom a match for the more advanced cars of the period, such as the low-slung $1\frac{1}{2}$ litre straight-eight Delage in 1927).

The first successful V-12 was built by Delage, and completed just in time for the 1923 French Grand Prix. But it was not until the engine was supercharged, in 1925, that it won important races, the French and Spanish Grands Prix.

A rival of the Delage was one of the great classic racing cars, the P2 Alfa Romeo, which had a career spanning nearly a decade. It had a supercharged straight-eight engine, designed by Vittorio Jano, and it is associated with some of the great names of motor racing, like Antonio Ascari, Guiseppe Cam-

pari, and Enzo Ferrari, as a driver and an entrant.

It was followed in 1932 by the even more famous P3 with which the Italian team had to meet the might of the German Mercedes-Benz and Auto-Union teams. The P3 was the epitome of the 'classic perpendicular' single-seater, and its lightness was some compensation for its modest power output of around 190 bhp from 2.6 litres. Enlarged to 3.8 litres to meet the German challenge, it was used by Nuvolari to win the 1935 German Grand Prix against tremendous odds.

The era of classic-shaped racing cars drew to a close with the 2.9 litre Maserati, the Alfa Romeo P3 and the Type 59 Bugatti, which was amongst the best-proportioned cars of the time. The Bugatti in particular exemplified the best features developed so laboriously in the 1920s, primarily a stiff chassis and firm non-independent springing, which was so soon to be overwhelmed by the advanced technology of the Germans.

The Auto-Union designed by Ferdinand Porsche had a 16 cylinder engine behind the driver, independent four wheel suspension, and a rigid, tubular frame. It used hydraulic brakes (pioneered by the 1921 Duesenberg, but seldom used between 1921 and 1934) and special alloys for strength and light-

Change. The engine compartment of the Type 158 Alfa Romeo looks very straightforward (top) compared with the complexity of a V-6 Ferrari, with its curling exhausts, spidery suspension and transmission casing.
Left: Lehoux (Alfa Romeo P3) leading Etancelin (Masserati 8C) in the 1934 Dieppe Grand Prix

ness. This was a step forward of enormous magnitude–it was a new dimension. Mercedes-Benz joined in with their less unconventional W25, which nevertheless emphasised that there was a whole new philosophy in racing car design.

The C-Type Auto-Union that followed was a development of Dr Porsche's original design, and the Mercedes-Benz W125 a refined W25, with a vastly more powerful engine. To say that these cars dominated Grand Prix racing would be an understatement. They remained technically outstanding for twenty years.

Milestones in motor racing have never since been quite so fundamental. There have been fewer breakthroughs in technique, fewer pioneers. Most of the important innovations had been achieved, and the important cars that followed were those exemplifying trends that motor racing in general was taking.

The ERA, developed from the Riley sports car pointed the way in 'voiturette' racing in the mid-1930s. The pinnacle in this class was the 'Alfetta', which was developed into the fabulous Type 158/159 Alfa Romeo of the post-war period. These cars composed the lower capacity end of the successful 1½ litre supercharged Formula after the war, along with the Maserati 4CLT, while the Talbot and eventually the 4½ litre Ferrari encompassed the upper end.

The 500 cc movement started in Britain not long after the war, and persisted for about 15 years. The cars were small motor cycle-engined single seaters, with tubular frames and power units behind the cockpits, partly because the engines were so light that they barely influenced the weight distribution and partly because it was convenient to drive the rear wheels by chain.

The Cooper was the most important, but there were dozens of different makes; some blossomed as manufacturers, but most vanished as quickly as they had appeared.

The 500 cc philosophy of budget motor racing was later expressed in Italy as Formula Junior, and while Formula 2 remained a very professional business, the bargain basement movement coalesced in this new, internationally recognised category of motor racing, built around cars using tuned production engines, rather than 'pure' racing units. In time, Formula Junior was superseded by Formula 3, on essentially similar lines.

Grand Prix cars continued much in the mould created by Mercedes-Benz before the war, and repeated in the 1950s with the W196, the last great racing car with a straight-eight engine. It had fuel injection, desmodromic valves, inboard brakes, a tubular space frame, and at first a streamlined body which proved of value only on very fast circuits (bodywork covering the wheels of Formula cars was subsequently banned). It had a companion sports car, the 300SLR, and during the 1954 and 1955 seasons both were tremendously successful.

The German team achieved a reputation for efficiency and advanced automotive engineering which continued to benefit their company for years afterwards.

The Vanwall took Britain into a leading position in Grand Prix racing for the first time since the 1920s. In this car aerodynamics were advanced to a point never before achieved before in open-wheeled single seaters. It also introduced Colin Chapman to the world of Formula 1, and brought the Constructors' Championship to Britain for the first time in 1958, although its drivers, Moss, Brooks and Schell, never won a title for themselves.

Left: German-American massive—the STP McNamara built for Andy Granatelli's team to compete at Indianapolis and other American paved oval tracks. Below, left: the smooth McLaren M16, with turbocharged Offenhauser engine, which Peter Revson drove into second place in the 1971 '500'. A derivative of this model, driven by Mark Donohue, won the race in the following year. Below: the low, lean look at Indianapolis in 1968, when the front row line-up was Bobby Unser's Offenhauser-powered car, and the Lotus turbines of Graham Hill and Joe Leonard

The Cooper 'grew up' from the subsidiary formulae, first with a front-engined design, then with a mid-engined car, in principle a copy of the 500 cc models. This first appeared in 1956 as a Formula 2 car, with a Coventry-Climax engine behind the driver, and a tubular space frame. It was a concept that every designer was soon imitating.

Lotus followed the lead with the Mark 18, then Ferrari with V-6 and V-8 Formula 1 cars. This was a motor racing milestone, as significant as Henry's Peugeot, but in 1962 came another development which allied a more advanced technology to the Coopers' intuition. Colin Chapman crystallised design with the Lotus 25 in the same way that Mercedes-Benz had nearly thirty years earlier. The Lotus discarded the space frame, and taking a lead from the aircraft industry introduced the built-up aluminium monocoque. With its V-8 engine, reclining driving position, and wide-based suspension layout, the Lotus 25 set the shape that racing cars were to follow for the next decade.

Detail changes followed. Most of them, like inboard suspension and side-mounted radiators, were pioneered by Chapman. Tony Rudd of BRM introduced the idea of stressing the engine as part of the monocoque in the abortive H-16 car, and the principle was happily adopted by Chapman for the Lotus 49. Aerodynamics played a growing role, and tyre width increased enormously. Four wheel drive came and went, but apart from a few radical novelties like turbine engines, the basic configuration of the Lotus 25 persisted thereafter.

One major departure from the clean cigar shape of the Lotus 25 came with the use of aerofoils, to press the car down on to the road and improve its grip on corners. These 'wings' grew excessively, until trimmed by regulations introduced following Graham Hill's and Jochen Rindt's spectacular double accident in the 1969 Spanish Grand Prix

Top: Jim Clark leading the 1964 French Grand Prix at Rouen in a Lotus-Climax; he lost the lead with a holed piston. Below: start of the 1968 United States Grand Prix at Watkins Glen, in the 'wings' era. Mario Andretti leads away from pole position in a Lotus 49, while eventual winner Jackie Stewart gets his Matra Ford off the line a few feet behind him

on the testing Montjuich circuit at Barcelona.

Alternative formulae were introduced within the framework of the FIA rules. 'Budget' racing appeared nationally and internationally in categories which in many cases meant cars retaining tubular space frames and using production-based engines and other components.

In America, the shadow of the pre-war Maserati 8CTF, the Grand Prix car built to challenge the Germans in the late 1930s, was meanwhile still cast over Indianapolis. Wilbur Shaw won the Memorial Day classic with the Boyle Special 8CTF in 1939, and again in 1940. He crashed while leading in 1941, and even in 1946 and 1947 the same car came third, and was fourth in 1948. Other 8CTF models did well, leading in 1949, and competing until 1951.

Widely different shapes. Emerson Fittipaldi in a sleek John Player Special acknowledges Ronnie Peterson, as he laps the Swedish driver's dumpy March 721X.
Below: Wilbur Shaw in the Maserati 8CTF 'Boyle Special' which set new standards at Indianapolis in the late 1930s.

As the 8CTF grew older, its influence waned. Its eight cylinder, supercharged 3 litre engine was eclipsed by the Offenhauser 'four' and in time independent front suspension went out of fashion in view of the specialised demands of the course. Transmissions became simplified because they were equal to the rolling start, and although disc brakes came into general use, they were relatively small.

Experiments with front wheel drive were short-lived, but engines were laid on their side to achieve low build, and by the early 1960s, Indy cars seemed in danger of becoming stereotyped, with specialisation reaching the stage where weight bias and even tyre treads were suited only to the long, left handed bends of the famous oval track.

Then, in 1961 along came Jack Brabham with his tiny Cooper, to be followed by Jim Clark and Dan Gurney with Chapman's brilliant Lotus. The image of the Lotus 25 had spread across the Atlantic, in the forms of the Indianapolis Types 29 and 38. Henceforward, the slim, mid-engined, all independently sprung racing car became the standard, world wide.

Great Names in Racing

The pages of racing history sparkle with the names of outstanding machines. Few constructors have been prominent in the sport for long periods: perhaps like Mercedes their policy has been to compete only spasmodically, but more often the effort of reaching the top and staying there has proved too demanding; some teams became almost permanent features of the scene, but like Cooper and Maserati just faded away; some slowly evolving lines of machinery have quite simply been overtaken by events, the Kurtis Indianapolis roadsters, for example.

Tradition counts for little, unless it goes hand in hand with results. Among the leading racing names of our time are some with histories going back decades, others which have appeared only very recently. . . .

Ferrari

When Enzo Ferrari was born in 1898, his father ran a small engineering works making sheds and other miscellaneous equipment for the state railway. Young Enzo was supposed to succeed to this modest business enterprise, but the First World War intervened. In 1916 his father and his brother Alfredo both died, and Enzo, a rather delicate soldier, was invalided out of the army, where he had served in a mountain artillery unit and spent part of the time shoeing mules.

For a man who was to make and break future champions, and have the rich and famous beating a path to his door, it was an inauspicious start. He eventually found work as a test driver, with a firm converting light trucks into cars, and then with CMN. This company had some sporting inclinations, and their test driver persuaded them to enter him in hill climbs and races. Thus he became the first driver to start in the first post-war race in Europe, the 1919 Targa Florio, run in November when snow lay on the Sicilian roads.

In 1920 he joined Alfa Romeo, and thereafter played a central role in racing. As a driver he achieved some good results, and after his drive in the Circuito del Savio at Ravenna in 1923 Count Baracca presented him with an emblem. This was the prancing horse which had been carried on the aircraft in which Baracca's son had died during the war. Ferrari adopted it for all his cars.

It was soon obvious that Ferrari's talent extended beyond driving, and he became increasingly involved in the management of Alfa Romeo racing affairs, to the point where he took over complete responsibility in 1929, under the banner Scuderia Ferrari. The team was enormously successful in Grand Prix and sports car racing, until the mighty German équipes forced a new pace in the mid-1930s.

The split with Alfa Romeo came in 1939. The company had taken direct control of its racing again, with Ferrari as team manager, in a back-to-the-wall fight against Auto-Union and Mercedes. But Ferrari was now quite unable to see eye to eye with the Alfa Romeo management, and left. He started his own company at Modena, nominally to

Left: Enzo Ferrari, enigmatic Italian, builder of some great cars. Above: Phil Hill in the Ferrari he shared with Belgian Olivier Gendebien to win at Le Mans in 1958. Right: the privately-owned 250LM Ferrari which won at Le Mans in 1965. In one of his rare sports car drives, Jochen Rindt shared the car with Masten Gregory.

make machine tools, although he completed his first two cars in time for the 1940 Mille Miglia; after the Second World War he started building cars in his own name. For these, Gioacchino Colombo designed the first of an extravagant V-12 engine, with which most Ferraris have been associated ever since.

Ferrari racing in the 1950s had its ups and downs. One of his sports cars won the first post-war Le Mans race, and in 1951 he beat the Alfa Romeos fairly and squarely in Grand Prix racing. In 1952

BRM variety. Left: the Mk 1 V-16, world-beater that never made the grade, driven here by Reg Parnell. Below: Vindication at Zandvoort. Jo Bonnier driving the 2½ litre four-cylinder car to victory in the 1959 Dutch Grand Prix at Zandvoort, cutting inside a tail-sliding Jack Brabham (Cooper-Climax) at the Hunzerug. Above: Graham Hill in a race he made his own. Five times winner of the Monaco Grand Prix at the Tabac in 1966, one year he failed to win, in a 2-litre intermediate BRM.

and 1953 Alberto Ascari took the world championship with Ferraris, then in 1956, with Mercedes-Benz once more out of the way, Fangio brought the title to Ferrari again, at the expense of falling out with the 'old man' for ever.

In 1958 Mike Hawthorn won the championship, and was followed by Ferrari drivers Phil Hill in 1961 and John Surtees in 1964. Ferraris have won more championship Grands Prix and Le Mans races than any other make, and throughout the teams have been presided over from a distance by the autocratic, huffy old man, mourning a son who died in his youth. Ferrari joined forces with Fiat–after a lifetime spent setting the pace in a cruel sport.

BRM

Probably the most enigmatic and controversial contender in Grand Prix history, BRM have competed in Grand Prix races longer than any other constructor except Ferrari. Together they have watched the passing of Alfa Romeo–Ferrari hastened this departure–Alta, Gordini, Talbot, Cooper, Vanwall, Maserati, Connaught, Aston Martin, Porsche, Honda, Eagle, and several other teams. But the two great British and Italian teams, in different ways both hangovers from a bygone age, have fought on almost continuously.

They have occasionally poked one another in the eye, without doing much real damage, while Cooper, Lotus, Matra, Brabham and the rest often picked up the real spoils of the game. Great drivers came and went. BRM arrived on the European circuits at the same time as Fangio. Graham Hill had barely got behind a wheel; Jackie Stewart was ten.

The BRM was conceived by Raymond Mays, and born out of the ashes of the pre-war ERA. The British motor industry, Mays reasoned, ought to be concerned with racing, if not individually then at least collectively. The old idea of racing for national prestige persisted.

If only it had been that simple. The resources of BRM at that time would have been barely sufficient to run a team of proprietary cars, far less design, build and develop a monumentally complicated vehicle like the BRM V-16. That engine itself, a a supercharged 1½ litre unit, was hardly the thing for a new team to cut its teeth on.

Mays had in any case miscalculated. His thinking was out of tune with the new age of racing. The whole British Motor Racing Research Trust eventually had to be sold; it was bought by Sir Alfred Owen, one of its earliest supporters.

The Press never forgave the V-16 BRM its opening debacle, at the Silverstone International Trophy race in 1951, when it lurched forward a yard or two, then stopped with a broken transmission. The V-16 was raced on after the formula to which it was built had been superseded, usually in British national races of little or no significance.

The team raced a Maserati for experience in the first seasons of the 2½ litre formula, and then at the end of 1955 brought out their own car. Whereas the V-16 had been complex, this was simple, it was more reliable and it was competitive. Yet somehow it never quite made the grade, even remained something of a bad joke. Not until 1959 did a BRM win a championship Grand Prix, and by then the Vanwall had gained the constructor's championship for Britain, and Cooper had become a force in racing.

Only after Sir Alfred Owen had issued a famous ultimatum, that unless it won races the team would be wound up, did BRM win the drivers' and constructors' championships. In 1962 the 1½ litre V-8 BRM gave the team, led by Graham Hill, its most successful season, and for the next three seasons it battled vigorously against Ferrari, Lotus and the rest.

Yet when the 3 litre formula came into force, BRM over-reached themselves once again. The lessons of their first car were ignored in an orgy of over-complication with an H-16 engine. The team won no more races until this was dropped–the only time the H-16 ever won it was in a Lotus.

The alternative was to develop the V-12 that BRM had thoughtfully laid down, but that took time, and for their next championship victory the team had to wait until 1970, when Pedro Rodriguez scored a resounding triumph in the Belgian Grand Prix at Spa.

For all its faults, the V-16 is an imperishable memory to all who heard it run in anger. The quaint, almost feudal way in which BRM arranged their affairs often irritated enthusiasts. Yet it was always an irritation of concern, not of scorn. BRM remained a team that people cared about. When it won, even its rivals applauded.

Lotus
Colin Chapman's Lotus company set the Grand Prix design pace through the 1960s–his Lotus 25 introduced monocoque construction, the 43 and 49 used engines as part of the structure, the 72 used torsion bar suspension, inboard brakes and side-mounted radiators. Chapman became recognized as one of the most radical designers in racing history, an innovator by any standards. His wedge-shaped cars, four-wheel drive cars, turbine-powered cars, lightweight monocoques, inboard suspension and novel detail work, successful or not, did more to change the philosophy of racing car design within ten years than all the novelties save one of the previous forty.

Lotus extremes. Left: in the beginning . . . there was C. Chapman in his quaintly-named Lotus 6, his first production model. Above: Seventeen years later, Lotus had won 42 Grands Prix; Jochen Rindt, motor racing's first posthumous champion, with the dramatic, wedge-shaped, torsion bar sprung, inboard braked Lotus 72

Colin Chapman began building trials cars as soon as he left London University in the late 1940s. A gifted driver as well as an engineer, he was soon racing the sports cars which followed the Austin Seven based trials machines, and selling replicas. In 1957 he built his first single-seater, the Lotus 12 Formula 2 car, which was powered by a 1½ litre Coventry Climax engine. He had already been called in as a design consultant by both BRM and Vanwall; he made considerable contributions to the competitivness of both cars, and greatly enhanced his reputation.

In parallel with this his Lotus company was growing, and established at its first real factory, at Cheshunt, where the world's first car to use a re-inforced glass fibre hull went into production in 1958. This was the successful, although relatively short-lived, Elite.

The first Grand Prix Lotus appeared in the same year. It was similar to the Formula 2 car, and Lotus sports cars, with its Coventry Climax engine mounted ahead of the cockpit. But within two years, Chapman followed the Cooper example in placing the engine behind the driver – this was the last important development in which he did not set the lead. Very soon he refined it, making the driver lie almost on his back, to reduce the car's frontal area.

In 1960 Stirling Moss gained the first Grand Prix win for the marque Lotus, with the rear-engined 18 at Monaco, and in the following year Innes Ireland took the first Grand Prix for Team Lotus, at Watkins Glen with the 21. Thus the works team was started on its way into a scintillating decade, when it won more drivers' and constructors' championships than any other team. By this time the team included a promising young Scot, who had raced against Chapman in an Elite – Jim Clark, with whom Team Lotus was to be identified for seven brilliant years.

Lotus cars took Clark to two world championships. He drove them in every type of racing, in a career which perhaps reached a peak when he won the 1965 Indianapolis 500 mile race, the first

time the Memorial Day classic had been won by a foreign driver since 1916.

Throughout the decade, Lotus designs set new standards, Chapman always providing the inspiration if not always detail design work, for he established an ambitious new factory at Hethel, in Norfolk. Lotus racing cars have been criticized for being 'too fragile', and by inference accident-prone or bad cars in which to have accidents, yet they won races consistently until their lean 1971 Grand Prix season. By that time Lotus had ceased selling racing cars, to concentrate on their road-going production models and their racing team, run in conjunction with the John Player tobacco company—even in this much-debated aspect of sponsorship, Colin Chapman had been a pace-setter.

Porsche

Dr Ferdinand Porsche designed cars for many years, yet his name never appeared on them. Back at the dawn of motoring there was an electric car called the Lohner-Porsche, but subsequent designs from his drawing boards at Austro-Daimler or his little design consultant's office in Stuttgart carried a variety of names. Among his creations were the Auto-Union Grand Prix cars, the Volkswagen, and the Tiger tank which gave the Allies so much trouble during the Second World War.

The first Porsche car was not made until 1948, in a small factory at Gmünd in Austria. The 356 was appropriately rear-engined and air-cooled and was a sort of sports Volkswagen. This small aero-dynamic coupé was soon successful in minor races and rallies, and by the time Ferdinand Porsche died in 1951 it was selling steadily.

In 1950 the business, which was controlled by Porsche's son Ferry, was moved to Zuffenhausen outside Stuttgart, where it has remained and grown. Under Ferry Porsche the policy was to spend money on racing, instead of pouring it into an advertising budget where it might not do any good.

This policy remained unchanged for years. Porsche found no need to change it. The editorial

Opposite: Jo Bonnier in the first Grand Prix Porsche cutting inside
Stirling Moss in Rob Walker's Lotus-Climax during the 1961 French
G.P. Above: two very different Porsche sports cars at Le Mans in 1971
The winning Marko-van Lennep 917, competing in the 24-hour race
for the last time, chasing the 911S coupe of Greub and Grant which
finished eighth in the GT category

copy gained from races and rallies, and the enhancement of the already strong marque loyalty which, far exceeded anything that could have have been achieved with an advertising budget. It put over most explicitly the message that Porsche road cars were fast, strong and competitive.

While early Porsche successes were obtained by private entrants, it was not long before Porsche began to race their cars, and to win their class at Le Mans and other long-distance classic events (the first Porsche class victory in the 24-hour race came in 1951, in the 1100 cc class). The 550 followed the 365, then came the RS and RSK, and with these

came the first outright victory for a Porsche in a major event, the 1956 Targa Florio (a race which was to see many Porsche triumphs in years to come).

In 1957 Ferry Porsche produced a $1\frac{1}{2}$ litre Formula 2 car, which was raced by several prominent drivers, among them Stirling Moss, Jean Behra, Jo Bonnier and Graham Hill. It won a number of races, particularly in 1960 with the Aintree 200 and the German Grand Prix, which was run under Formula 2 rules and did not count for the world championship that year.

The following year these Formula 2 cars were uprated to race in the $1\frac{1}{2}$ litre Grands Prix, when the works drivers were Dan Guney and Jo Bonnier. However, Porsche won only one championship Grand Prix, the 1961 French event, with their definitive Grand Prix car, which had an eight-cylinder horizontally-opposed engine, air-cooled of course.

After this, the factory concentrated on rallies and prototype or sports car racing. They won the Monte Carlo Rally three years in succession (1968–70); in racing they were runners-up in the International Manufacturers' Championship for two years, then won it outright for the first time in 1969 (having already won the 2-litre category six times in a row). This was the year which saw the introduction of the 917, a fabulous machine with a flat-12 air-cooled engine.

These cars won nearly 40 major international sports car races before the prototype regulations were changed, and the 917 outlawed.

Brabham

Jack Brabham brought a new style to Grand Prix racing. His active career spanned 23 years, and only at the age of 44 did he decide to retire, to give more time to his family.

Brabham started racing midget cars in Australia, where he acquired the 'tail-out' style of driving that characterised him for years. He came to Europe to race a Cooper-Bristol which was something between a sports car and a Grand Prix car, for a tentative season in 1955. He was a dogged, rather than keen, rival for the established teams at a time when the Mercedes-Benz team led by Fangio ruled the circuits.

In 1957 he became a full member of the Cooper works team, and together they led the trend towards cars with engines behind the drivers. In the mid-1950s, Brabham's approach was novel; it came as

something of a shock for the establishment to find that the taciturn Australian could achieve results by 'tuning' the chassis *as well as* the engine. He was one of the first drivers to employ suspension adjustments so that the car, and not the driver, did the work.

Brabham's technique was to calm the car rather than fight it, and he did this to such effect that he won the world championship in the unlikely looking Cooper-Climax of 1959. The following year he did it again, with victories in the Dutch, Belgian, French, British and Portuguese Grands Prix. Then, at the height of his success, he astonished the motor racing world by leaving Cooper to build and race his own cars in 1962.

The new Brabham cars, engineered by Brabham himself in conjunction with Ron Tauranac, were successful in subsidiary classes, particularly in Formula 2 with Honda engines, but at first Brabham had little success in Grand Prix racing.

In 1966, with the change to 3 litres, Brabham introduced an essentially 'interim' model using an Australian Repco engine, which was basically an adaptation of an American Buick V-8. By the standards most pundits had predicted for the new formula, the Brabhams were too small, too light, and under-powered. But at a time when many people had dismissed Brabham's 1959 and 1960 Championships as flukes, Brabham won a third world title.

His back-up driver, New Zealander Denny Hulme, won the Championship in 1967, but with a developed version of the Repco engine, Brabham himself struck a lean patch in 1968 and 1969. Then with the Ford-Cosworth engine, his straightforward Grand Prix cars once again became race winners, and but for ill-luck he would have been in a strong position to challenge for a fourth championship in the BT33.

Meanwhile, Brabham cars continued to be strong contenders in other single-seater classes, at times seeming to be mainstays of Formula 2, Formula 3 and Formula B. In America Brabham had, of course, pioneered European participation at Indianapolis, and the Cooper which he raced in the 1961 500 started a revolution in the design of American track racing cars.

With 14 Grand Prix wins to his credit, Jack Brabham hung up his helmet at the end of 1970. Perhaps surprisingly, he also broke the direct ties

Left: Jack Brabham, the quiet Australian who survived 23 years of motor racing. Opposite: breasting a rise in his own car at the Nürburgring during the German Grand Prix in 1966, the year he won his third driver's championship

with his company, but the line of cars bearing his name continued.

Jack was still at the top of his form when he retired, still a stern adversary on the circuits, difficult to overtake and a supreme tactician. He was awarded the OBE after winning the championship in a car bearing his own name. He set his stamp on motor racing as the man who mastered cars.

Ford

Motor racing is an activity where some general rules simply do not apply–it is unlike many types of engineering, for example, where if enough money is poured in, almost anything can be achieved. In motor racing, the fundamental objective–winning races–cannot be achieved with any certainty, and championships are elusive things. Ford found out the facts for themselves.

Henry Ford dabbled in motor sport with some brutally primitive devices in the early days of motoring, but thereafter his company showed only spasmodic interest in competition, until the 1960s. During that decade, it made great efforts on most fronts, from drag racing to international rallies.

This effort started in NASCAR stock car racing, then moved on to the great road and track events. At first the impetus came from America, and was then taken up by Ford of Britain.

In 1963 Indianapolis was the target, Ford providing the engines, Lotus the cars and the principal driver, Jim Clark. They came within a whisper of success, frustrated by a few pints of another driver's oil, and had to wait until 1965 for victory in the 500, when Clark won at 150.686 mph.

Meanwhile, Ford launched an assault on European motor racing, for reasons of prestige and publicity in the most ancient traditions of the sport. Their main target was Le Mans, but they entered

Opposite, top: Mike Hawthorn at Aintree in 1957 with a V-8 Ferrari, a Lancia shorn of its side tanks, which he placed third in the British Grand Prix. Opposite, below: 1971 champion driver Jackie Stewart in the 1971 champion car, the Tyrrell-Ford. Left: classic sports racing car—John Surtees swooping through a Nürburgring dip in a P3 Ferrari. Below: front row moving off at the start of the 1965 British Grand Prix. Clark, on pole position with a Lotus 33, won after a great race with Hill, second on the front row with his BRM; Richie Ginther was third-fastest in the 12-cylinder Honda, while Stewart, nearest the camera, placed his BRM fifth

other sports car races and saloon car racing, and less directly single-seater racing through their engines. Twice Ford came near to putting their name on the front of a Grand Prix car; the first was the four-wheel drive Cosworth, the second eventually emerged as the Tyrrell-Ford.

It took Ford three years, and a fortune in time, money and materials, to win at Le Mans. They tried to buy Ferrari, lock stock and barrel, but eventually decided to challenge him. This involved a whole string of cars, painfully developed from Eric Broadley's Lola GT of 1963, and eventually for this one race a huge mobile workshop, the personnel of a small factory, and 27 tons of spares and components imported into France for the occasion. The latest space-age techniques were used, and the best materials available. Ford employed drivers of the calibre of Graham Hill, Bruce McLaren, Ken Miles and Chris Amon.

After two years of harsh disappointment, Ford won. In 1966 McLaren and Amon took the 24-hour classic in a Mk 2 GT40, becoming the first drivers ever to cover more than 3,000 miles in the event. Ford won again the next year, with an even more massive effort which included six cars; one of the two which survived was first, driven by A. J. Foyt and Dan Gurney, to give Ford an all-American triumph.

John Wyer's Gulf-sponsored team of GT40s won the race in the next two years, and in 1968 gained the sports car championship in the name of Ford. By this time the Dearborn company was withdrawing from racing.

Meanwhile, Ford of Britain had given Cosworth Engineering a commission. 'Build us an engine to win Grand Prix races,' it said, 'it is worth £100,000'.

Cosworth

Keith Duckworth worked for Lotus, until his independent nature prevailed. Together with Mike Costin, he set up a new firm to make racing engines, Cosworth Engineering. Because the Ford Anglia engine held considerable promise for tuners, notably excellent 'breathing' characteristics, they embarked on a programme to develop it for Formula Junior in 1959.

Its outstanding success in this class attracted the attention of Ford, who in 1962 offered Duckworth a token payment toward the development costs of a 1 litre Formula 2 engine also based on the Anglia.

In time, another Formula 2 engine followed, for the 1600 cc formula. This was the FVA (Four Valve series A), which was a step towards a more ambitious project–a Grand Prix engine.

When the 3 litre Formula was introduced in 1966, most British teams were left without a suitable engine. The practice of using proprietary engines had grown up with the availability of competitive Coventry Climax units, but they had withdrawn from racing, and of the British teams only BRM were in a position to develop their own engines. These they were prepared to sell, but unhappily elected to build the H-16.

Left: Ford GT40 at Daytona, 1967. Pit work in long-distance races can often be decisive. Right: Keith Duckworth and Harley Copp of Ford with a Cosworth FVA engine, the four-cylinder prototype of the DFV 3 litre Grand Prix power unit. Below: another of Duckworth's brain-children, the four-wheel drive Grand Prix car. It never raced, for the design principle was overtaken by racing cars with aerofoils, which gave two-wheel drive machines an adequate grip on the road

The complication and weight of this engine were against it, and apart from BRM only Lotus used it. Ford came to the rescue of British constructors by commissioning Duckworth to make a Formula 1 engine. This was the Cosworth DFV (Double Four Valve), based on two FVAs to make a V-8. It was to become one of the most successful Grand Prix engines of all time.

At first it was used exclusively by Lotus, who had a close association with Ford, and the engine carried FORD on its cam covers. Chapman designed it into the chassis structure of the Lotus 49, and Jim Clark drove it to victory in its first race, the 1967 Dutch Grand Prix.

By the following year it was also in McLaren and Matra chassis, then in Brabhams when the Repco was over-stretched, then in March, Surtees and Tyrrell chassis. BRM, Eagle and Ferrari soldiered on with their own power units. Cooper used an old Maserati engine and subsequently a BRM V-12, but went out of business.

The product of Keith Duckworth's genius remained virtually unbeatable long after it should have gone into decline in the face of the twelve-cylinder opposition.

Tyrrell

From a timber business in Surrey, and a reputation for talent-spotting, Ken Tyrrell took on the world in motor racing. He once drove in races himself, but decided in 1956 that he had not enough talent and took to entering cars instead. Bruce McLaren, John Surtees, Tony Maggs, John Love, Jacky Ickx, François Cevert, and Jean-Pierre Beltoise were among the drivers who started in the Big Time with Ken Tyrrell, but the turning point that was to lead him into Formula 1, and towards a world championship award with his own name on it, came in 1964.

Looking for a new driver for his Cooper-BMC Formula 3 team, Tyrrell asked the little known Jackie Stewart to take a test drive at Goodwood, the Sussex circuit which was later abandoned for racing. Stewart was signed that afternoon, carried all before him in Formula 3, showed his ability in Formula 2 before the end of the season, and was snapped up by BRM for Formula 1 in 1965.

The Tyrrell-Stewart partnership was renewed for Formula 2, and together they shepherded Matra into Grand Prix racing. Driving Tyrrell's Matra-International Ford-Cosworth engined cars, Stewart won the World Drivers' Championship in 1969.

In the following year, however, Matra decided to race only their own V-12 engines, which left Ken Tyrrell without a suitable car. He started the

'Honestly Ken . . .' Jackie Stewart explains track conditions to Ken Tyrrell, who doesn't seem to believe him

season with the new March 701, but decided that if he was to keep Jackie Stewart with him, he must provide the right machinery. Accordingly, he set out to build his own cars.

This was one of motor racing's best-kept secrets. Designer Derek Gardner worked in his own home, and components for the first Tyrrell-Ford were acquired surreptitiously. The car appeared in the late summer of 1970, won nothing but was developed to raceworthiness. In 1971 Tyrrell won the constructors' championship.

Ken Tyrrell is big, bluff and blunt. His partnership with Stewart has turned out to be one of the most formidable in racing. With the bossy authority of a Neubauer and the instinct for motor racing of a Ferrari, coupled with lively humour and great charm, Tyrrell took on teams with apparently more resources than he could ever hope to muster in a Surrey timber yard – and won.

Offenhauser

The Offenhauser story is of a dynasty rather than of racing engine design. It is a story without end so far as racing in the United States is concerned. . . .

The title the engine ought to carry is even debatable, for many famous names have been

caught up in its history. But it is as the 'Offy', largely the brainchild of Fred Offenhauser, that the classic twin overhead camshaft engine with its famous barrel crankcase is best known.

Offenhauser was born of German immigrant parents in 1888, and became a talented and painstaking engineer. During the First World War, Bob Burman turned to Harry Miller's Master Carburettor Company in Los Angeles for a copy of his 1913 Peugeot engine; Offenhauser was the manager of Miller's works, and under his supervision the Miller-built engine was a big improvement on the original.

The next milestone came when Leo Goossen joined Miller, to design an eight-cylinder version of the Peugeot 'four'. Features of this design were twin overhead camshafts, four valves per cylinder, prism-shaped combustion chambers and the massively strong barrel crankcase. Offenhauser adopted Henry's piston-type cam followers when he saw a

Turbocharged Offy. The oldest engine in racing in its exhaust-boosted form—special engines built for Indianapolis qualifying have given 'flash' dynamometer readings approaching 1000 bhp

racing Ballot in 1919, and the pattern of the engine was established.

Goossen embarked on a four-cylinder version of this engine for a racing speed boat in 1927, and within a few years this was adopted for cars. In 1933 Miller's firm became bankrupt, and Offenhauser, to whom Miller was already heavily in debt, acquired the stock-in-trade, and carried on making the engine.

In 1934 the four-cylinder Offenhauser was firmly established as the premier Indianapolis engine – a hard-won title, which was not to be lightly relinquished. The big 220 cu in (3.6 litre) four had begun a career that was to span more than 40 years.

The business went on through the Second World War, until 1946 when Offenhauser handed it over to Louis Meyer and Dale Drake as a gift.

Meyer's career as a driver included winning the

Indy 500 three times; his partner was a former valve-spring manufacturer who had once been his riding mechanic. Meyer-Drake Engineering carried on developing the old engine, with Goossen still at the drawing board.

The engine grew up, changed size, was built in light alloy instead of cast iron, and after Meyer had joined Ford, acquired an exhaust-driven turbocharger. Evolution raised the power over the years to around 800 bhp in Indy qualifying trim. Regularly, throughout its racing career, heads wagged again and again – 'The old Offy really has shot its bolt this time'.

It never has.

Ladder to the Top

The easiest way into motor racing as a driver is to have a lot of money. This is as true in the 1970s as it was at the turn of the century. The difference is that in the early years of motor racing it was almost essential to have a lot of money; later it became merely desirable. Also, the way to the top need no longer be so direct. Once upon a time there was only one sort of motor racing, and you either took part in it, or you took part in no motor racing at all. Not only has 'The Top' since taken on a number of different meanings, but the ways to it are now graduated.

The important thing to recognise is that while rewards at the summit of the sport are large, in some cases very large indeed, amounting to an annual income for a world champion class driver of well over £100,000 a year, there is still no certain way of driving talent achieving recognition. Stories of enthusiastic youngsters who are 'discovered' by avuncular team managers are not unknown, but in fact, very few drivers ever get into the picture without years of effort, disappointment, and low income. Like any branch of show business, for every one who makes the grade, hundreds do not, and there are legions of disillusioned young men who are poorer, and perhaps wiser, for having tried.

Yet having said all that, there can be few more exciting and glamorous ways of life, and if the

'Prentice hands. Start of a Formula Junior race at Goodwood in 1960. Several of the drivers became stars—on the front row are two future world champions, Jim Clark and John Surtees

Formula Ford. Close racing in Cortina-engined cars is excellent training for aspiring drivers.
Right: pre-war voiturettes at London's Cyrstal Palace – Bira in the White Mouse stable's ERA 'Romulus' leading two more ERAs

investment is available, a season or two in one of the lower grades of racing, like Formula Ford or Formula Vee, working on a tight budget, with little more equipment than a set of tools, an old van, and a trailer to carry the racing car, can be rewarding to any young man. It will either disabuse him of the idea that he is cut out to be a racing driver, or talent will shine through, and he might acquire the confidence, even perhaps the cash to take the next step.

But what constitutes the first step?

This depends greatly on the money available. It need only be enough to build a racing car in the back yard, and enter club races. The car can in fact be a saloon, or a sports car, or one of the elementary single seaters, mostly designed round production engines of one sort or another for which spares are easy to get and cheap. Membership of a motor club is essential, and of a national automobile club in order to obtain the necessary competition licence.

Ideally, if the cash is available, the best course for a novice is to enter one of the nationally or internationally recognised categories of racing. He can go for single seaters, with Volkswagen, Ford, Fiat or Renault engines, and will find that in most countries the cost of one of these cars will work out at around the price of a better-class road-equipped sports car, or a good luxury saloon.

Schools for racing drivers have been established in many countries. Most are commercial enterprises, and charge fees, but they will also sometimes supply cars and enter drivers in races as part of the course of tuition. They are useful for gauging ability before buying a car, and starting motor racing safely. Many famous drivers are products of motor racing schools.

The cost of a season's racing depends upon how many races a driver does, and the avoidance of major breakdowns or crashes. Insurance for racing car crash damage can be bought, but premiums are necessarily high, and they will not cover mechanical trouble.

A season's budget will also depend on whether the aspiring ace has a job which he needs to attend during the week, and whether he races abroad or only in his own country. It depends on whether he needs to employ a mechanic (full or part time) or whether he can do all the work on his car by himself. Most amateurs enlist friends whom they do not have to pay.

Part of the investment in the racing team will be in the form of a van, or a trailer for the racing car. Spare engines in amateur racing are generally a luxury, but a major and unavoidable expense will be tyres. Racing cars consume tyres at a much greater rate than road cars, and the tyres are much

more expensive. Even in Formula Ford, which specifies road tyres, competitive race performances make heavy demands on rubber, and this is an area where severe financial strictures may not pay off.

Likely income from racing, at least in the early stages of the game can for most purposes be ignored. Unless a ready-made philanthropist is quickly available the money to be made is negligible. But it brings us to the question of sponsorship. This is an arrangement in which a commercial firm pays for a proportion of the racing programme (not necessarily in cash) in return for certain considerations or services. These will include display of the firm's name while racing, or the occasional use of the racing car for exhibition or promotional purposes. It may mean the driver making appearances at a showroom, or giving talks on motor racing to promote a product, or any number of things.

In the amateur grades of racing, such sponsorship is most likely to come from a local garage or accessory shop. It also depends for its continuance on a certain amount of results in the field, and the driver or team manager sticking to his part of the bargain, and giving the sponsor value for his money.

Income from prize money will not be substantial, even for a successful Formula Ford, Vee, Renault or Fiat driver. There are however, trade bonuses and cash prizes from sponsored championships available for winning, or gaining places. They are usually dependent on employing a certain component or product, and displaying the appropriate decal on the racing car, and perhaps the transporter as well.

Having·successfully passed the hurdles of a season or two in one form of amateur racing or another, the novice will probably look for either a semi-professional drive, or go along to a sponsor with the chance of more substantial financial assistance. In Europe he is likely to use this to enter an international category, such as Formula 3 or the 2 litre sports car class.

He can choose from a variety of classes, like Formula Atlantic in Britain, or Formula B in the United States. In any case, he will be in a faster car, demanding more professional preparation, and a greater degree of skill at the wheel. The competition will almost certainly be tougher, and the dangers greater. Plainly, the higher the speeds people race at, the graver the possible consequences of an accident, and the more circumspect drivers must be in their choice of safety equipment.

Formula 3 races are closely fought, and represent

Formula 3 tension and excitement (above) as a field races up from Abbey Curve at Silverstone in a tight competitive line. Tensions released (below) after two cars touched at Cyrstal Palace, one driver punched the other in a fury. The RAC held an enquiry . . .

Formula 2 is often more competitive than Formula 1—the cars are closely matched, and many of the drivers are on the threshold of Formula 1, or already racing in the Grands Prix. At Mallory Park in 1972 (above) Argentinian Carlos Reutemann in a Brabham leads Swede Ronnie Peterson in a March and South African Jody Scheckter in a McLaren

severe tests for a young driver. But some at least, for example the race that traditionally precedes the Monaco Grand Prix, are conducted not only in front of the top team managers in the business, but also before the assembled might of the world's motor racing Press. This can be daunting, because a good performance here will bring a driver to the notice of the Press faster than several wins elsewhere, and could be very important to him indeed.

There is no certain way of getting the Press on your side, or becoming recognised as a talented driver except to excel at the wheel. Journalists can be primed to look out for a driver, and will not be slow in writing favourable reports, because it is a feather in a journalist's cap if he spots promising drivers early. On the other hand journalists are not as a rule easy to convince, and no amount of hard-luck stories will persuade them that a driver has real ability if he remains at the back of the field.

The value of getting into Formula 2 is that it is the only single-seater category where a driver can match his talent against the stars without actually competing in Formula 1. The list of European Formula 2 Champions is studded with drivers who graduated into Formula 1 (Jackie Stewart never won the title, but he so overwhelmed Formula 3 in 1964 that BRM snapped him up before he had a chance to take the next step up the ladder—he jumped two rungs).

History shows that if a driver has natural ability, it will show quite early in his career. He may persevere, and gain recognition more slowly, but the drivers who won most Grands Prix, Clark, Fangio, Stewart, Moss, achieved complete superiority in each category of racing as their careers progressed. This is the mark of a great, natural driver as opposed to one who has to fight hard to shave those fractions off a lap time. These are the drivers who made it look easy when leading a race, yet always had speed in hand.

Nobody can precisely specify the qualities a driver needs. Besides good visual acuity, a keen sense of balance, the right temperament (whatever it is), the appropriate mixture of courage and self-control, he also needs ambition, dedication, and an ability to get on well with people. Charming the best efforts out of mechanics and suppliers is as important for a potential world champion as cutting a dash on the track. He needs emotional control, large reserves of concentration, and a capacity for enduring disappointment.

Thousands of hopeful drivers compete in hundreds of motor races the year round, at scores of tracks throughout the world. But they can only become world champion one at a time.

Great Drivers

In motor racing, as in so many other activities, greatness is not measured simply in terms of results. *How* drivers raced cars counts for at least as much as how *fast* they drove them. Throughout racing history the truly great drivers have been those who could influence the course of a race, who were able to gain advantage from positions of disadvantage.

The great drivers have not always been the top scorers, and some have been the tragedians of motor racing, like the Mexican Rodriguez brothers, both dedicated to racing, but both destined to die at the wheel. They left their marks as drivers of special calibre; they drove racing cars with absolute determination, with bravery, and with an urge to succeed so strong that they mastered situations when, by rights, they should have admitted defeat.

Spectators can tell when a driver is putting in an extra effort, squeezing a little more speed from his car at points on a circuit to cut his lap times by fractions of a second. They can see when the ultimate loads are being applied to the suspension, and sense that tyres are on the threshold of losing their grip on the road. There is a set about a car, and while there is a smoothness in its progress which shows that the driver's judgment is still precise, he is clipping the track edge by an inch instead of a foot, braking deeper into corners, changing gear faster, 'keeping his foot in it'—driving his car to the limit.

This is the point where artistry can be seen in motor racing, this is where some drivers, by their courage, or their skill, eyesight or sense of balance—

Opposite, top: Jim Clark driving a Lotus 49 in the 1968 British Grand Prix at Silverstone, on his way to his fifth British victory in six years, and sadly his last. His 1968 team mate Graham Hill surveys the gleaming new Lotus 49 on the starting grid for its second race, the Belgian Grand Prix.
Below: Juan Manuel Fangio, five times world champion, at speed in the last great straight-eight Grand Prix car, the W196 Mercedes-Benz

a combination of talents – can be singled out. They are the members of the sporting elite who whatever the conditions will try to jump higher, run faster, or throw further than anyone else.

Juan Manuel Fangio, five times Champion Driver of the World, drove the winning car in 24 Grands Prix. None was more dramatic or memorable than the last, the German Grand Prix of 1957.

The Nürburgring circuit twists and dives and loops through the wooded slopes of the Eifel mountains in north-west Germany. It is the longest circuit in the world regularly used for racing, with a lap distance of 14.7 miles, and a reputed 172 corners, 88 left-handed and 84 right-handed. It is a supreme test for a driver, demanding concentration, skill, and courage.

In 1957, the British racing renaissance was gathering momentum. Hawthorn, Moss, Collins and Brooks had won Grands Prix, and it was obviously only a matter of time before one of them won the World Championship. The Vanwall had shown the winning form that was to gain the newly-instituted Manufacturers' Championship in 1958. BRM had won their first Continental race, albeit a minor one, at Caen. Could the Latin sun that had been shining on motor racing for so long – it seemed like a generation – at last be setting?

It was heading for eclipse, but before this came, Fangio in his Maserati taught the upstart Anglo-Saxons a sharp lesson.

The Vanwall team stumbled at that German Grand Prix meeting in 1957. Suspension settings for the smooth asphalt of Aintree and Silverstone were hopelessly inadequate for the punishing bumps of the Nürburgring. Moss, Brooks and the young Stewart Lewis-Evans were pitched and bounced around in their cockpits, and to all intents and purposes handicapped out of the race before it started.

The V-8 Ferraris had by this time lost most outward signs of their Lancia ancestry, and the team was anxious for success. Their Maserati rivals had a revised version of the classic 250F in 1957, lighter and sleeker, which Fangio had driven to win the first three rounds of the championship, while the Ferraris had been second and third in the French Grand Prix, and second and third to a Vanwall in the British Grand Prix at Aintree.

At Nürburgring the two Italian teams were ranged against each other. On the front row of the grid were two cars of each marque: Fangio (Maserati) on pole position, alongside him Mike Hawthorn (Ferrari), Frenchman Jean Behra (Maserati), and Peter Collins (Ferrari). On the row behind, Tony Brooks (Vanwall), Harry Schell (Maserati) and Stirling Moss (Vanwall) promised pursuit, but on the basis of practice times not challenge, for Fangio and Hawthorn had been a clear 10 seconds a lap faster in practice. The race for the lead was obviously going to be a straight fight, Ferrari versus Maserati.

The Ferraris had one distinct advantage. They could go through the race, 22 laps of the difficult circuit, 311 miles, without refuelling and probably without changing tyres. The Maseratis, on the other hand, would certainly need to change their rear tyres, so team manager Ugolini sought compensation, and decided to start his cars with half-empty fuel tanks. These could be topped up when the wheels were changed at around half-distance.

In practice Fangio had shattered his old lap record, but in the race he was going to need to repeat his pole position time every lap – three and a half hours of very hard work in the heat of summer for a man of 45.

As the flag fell, Hawthorn and Collins took their Ferraris into the lead, intent on pressing home the advantage they already had, the ability to run through the race non-stop. Fangio tailed them, measuring them up, while on the second lap Hawthorn set a new lap record in 9 minutes 37.9 seconds (a speed of 88.24 mph). Fangio replied by cutting almost five seconds from this time, and as the cars roared through the South Curve just after the start line, he overtook Collins.

He caught and passed Hawthorn in a series of downhill swerves, and was five seconds ahead of the Ferrari driver when he completed the fourth lap. Getting the bit between his teeth, Fangio went faster and faster, opening the gap to the pursuing Ferraris to nearly half a minute as he cut the record again and again. The Old Man gave an astonishing display of skill, clipping fractions here, braking late there, and judging every one of those 172 corners with a precision which left the spectators gasping.

On lap 10 he broke nine and a half minutes for the first time, and on lap 12 he pulled his sizzling Maserati into the pits for the tyre change. But the mechanics got in each other's way as they jacked up the car, and muddled the replacement wheels, so that almost a minute passed before Fangio could restart. In a little more than half that time the Ferrari drivers gobbled up the margin Fangio had gained so painfully, and swept past, back into the lead.

The Argentinian's face was set firm beneath his battered brown helmet as he burst back into the race, for the arithmetic was inescapable. He was almost a minute behind, with ten laps to go. In the first ten laps of the race he had gained half a minute; to gain at almost twice that rate in the next ten appeared impossible. As if to confirm this, Peter Collins threw in a new lap record as he took his

German Grand Prix, 1957. The hares (above) Mike Hawthorn and Peter Collins. The hound (below), Fangio in his Maserati. A pit stop meant that he had to drive the race of his life to win this classic

Ferrari into the lead from team mate Hawthorn.

Fangio now had fresh tyres and a new fuel load, so predictably he gained nothing on the two Ferraris during the next two laps. But his manager, Marcello Giambertone, realized that this would be so, and suggested that it could be turned to advantage—Tavoni, in charge of the Ferrari pits, might be lulled into over-confidence. He might, suggested Giambertone, think that Fangio was in trouble.

Sure enough, Tavoni signalled Collins and Hawthorn to maintain a steady speed, and save their cars. But the lap distance at the 'Ring meant that drivers were out of contact with their pits for nearly ten minutes, and once a driver has been given a signal, his team manager had no means of countermanding it until he completes another lap. So if Fangio was ordered to speed up only as he started on a lap, he would complete it before the rival pits noticed, and as he would still pass the pits *after* Collins and Hawthorn, they would have to complete another lap before their pit could tell tham to speed up.

Fangio had one lap to speed up, and another lap before Tavoni could warn his drivers that the gap was closing—28 miles of racing before Collins and Hawthorn could be alerted to look in their mirrors. Fangio started his attack on lap 14, immediately cutting into the Ferrari drivers' lead. On lap 18 the gap was down to 20 seconds. Fangio had broken the 90 mph lap barrier at the 'Ring.

Fangio after his epic drive at the Nürburgring in 1957. It was the last and probably the greatest of his 24 Grand Prix wins

In vain Tavoni hung out the FASTER signal. On lap 20 Fangio was only three seconds behind the Ferrari pair, and had put in his tenth record lap of the day, in an almost incredible time of 9 minutes 17.4 seconds – 91.53 mph.

Hawthorn now led, Collins on his tail, both driving on the limit to fight off this unexpected Maserati challenge. Fangio moved in for the kill, passing Collins, who briefly repassed, and setting out after Hawthorn. Mike fought back hard, but on this day there was no holding Fangio, who stormed on to win by 3.6 seconds.

His speed, 88.79 mph, was faster than the 1956 lap record, and in winning he consolidated his lead in the 1957 Drivers' Championship, which he was to win with 40 points to Stirling Moss' 25. This was his last, and greatest, Championship race victory; afterwards he admitted: 'I don't ever want to drive like that again'. The following year he retired, leaving the history of motor racing richer.

Jim Clark, sadly, did not live to retire. He died at the wheel of a Lotus Formula 2 car in an unimportant race at Hockenheim in West Germany in April 1968. Earlier that year, in South Africa, he had surpassed Fangio's record of Grand Prix victories, and his prospects for the mainstream European season were brilliant. . . .

Team Lotus spent much of the 1967 season achieving reliable raceworthiness in the pace-setting 49, and had the strongest driver combination on the circuits, Jim Clark and Graham Hill. Clark had driven the 49 to win its first race, the Dutch Grand Prix in June, but won only one other race, the British Grand Prix, before the teams gathered at Monza for the Italian Grand Prix in September.

The natural genius of Jim Clark was reaching its zenith, and he already had two world championships and a score of Grand Prix victories behind him. Thirty-one years old, he was adored not only by enthusiastic spectators, but by their mums and dads at home, who recognized his unaffected good nature. Graham Hill was even then approaching veteranship – a fiercely determined driver, without the same gifts as Clark, but the living proof that there are some men with the resolution to do almost anything to which they set their minds.

The 49 was unquestionably the fastest thing on the tracks. It started from pole position in every race from its introduction throughout 1967, yet victory often eluded it – Team Lotus almost seemed robbed by ill-fortune, as their green and yellow cars retired or fell back with trifling faults (this was the last year the Lotus works cars wore their traditional colours; not until 1968 were they painted to look like cigarette packets).

The Italian Grand Prix was crucial, for there would be only two other races, the American and Mexican Grands Prix, to settle the championship. As the European season reached its Monza climax, Denny Hulme was forging ahead in the drivers' championship, and the Repco-engined Brabhams in the constructors' championship.

Brabham drivers Brabham and Hulme went to Monza with four wins in eight races behind them, strongly placed. The Ferrari team, on the other hand, was enfeebled. Lorenzo Bandini had died at Monaco, and Enzo Ferrari had said that there were no more 'professional' drivers in Italy, so for the Italian Grand Prix Chris Amon was entered in a solitary 12-cylinder car. Dan Gurney had driven his Eagle to victory in the Belgian Grand Prix, and went strongly in practice at Monza. John Surtees' season had not been very satisfactory with the Honda; the car was far too heavy, but the team came to Italy with their powerful V-12 installed in a new monocoque hull. This had been built in six weeks at the Surtees factory in Slough, hard by the Lola works. Surtees had a long association with Lola, and although Honda protested that the new car was a Honda, its Lola characteristics stretched

credibility. Not too much was expected of it at Monza, because there had been time for only a few test laps at Goodwood.

Clark made the fastest lap in practice, 1 minute 28.5 seconds, almost four seconds inside the record, which stood to the 1966 winner, Ludovico Scarfiotti. He had driven a Ferrari, to become the first Italian driver to win the race since Alberto Ascari in 1952.

Beside Clark on the front row of the grid were Jack Brabham (Brabham-Repco) and Bruce McLaren, whose McLaren had a BRM V-12 engine. In the row behind were Chris Amon and Dan Gurney, then came Denny Hulme in the second Brabham, Jackie Stewart in the uncertain BRM H-16, and Graham Hill in the second Lotus 49. Surtees was on the fourth row, together with Scarfiotti (Eagle).

The start was chaotic. Most Grands Prix were by this time started from a 'dummy' grid, where the cars assemble short of the actual start line, then drivers start their engines and move up to the starter, and it was the Italian organisers' intention to use this system. The field dutifully assembled, and a man with a little green flag carefully beckoned them towards the line, where the starter began to ascend his rostrum. Unfortunately, he had waited too long. He should have started his job with 30 seconds to go, but waited until nearly 20 had passed.

Some drivers simply assumed that after all the dummy grid system was not to be used—there had been no drivers' briefing. Brabham let in his clutch, and lit off down the track, momentarily

Slipstreaming at Monza in the 1967 Italian Grand Prix. John Surtees, the eventual winner in a new Honda, rushes into the Parabolica ahead of Chris Amon (Ferrari), Bruce McLaren (McLaren) and Jochen Rindt (Cooper)

glancing sideways to make sure he was not alone.

He was not. Bruce McLaren heard the Brabham engine note rising, and followed suit almost at once. Clark was watching the official starter, and he only realized what was happening when he saw Brabham disappearing, his back tyres wreathed in smoke. Gurney swerved round McLaren, Amon over-revved. The race was on, and the starter was left to wave his flag feebly as the cars blasted towards the Curva Grande in a welter of noise.

Brabham's lead was short-lived. Gurney had been as quick off the mark as the Australian, and

The two Lotus drivers fought out the lead with Brabham and Hulme, while the rest dropped back, or began to fall out.

On lap 11 it was obvious that something was wrong with Clark's Lotus, for he slowed and was caught by his pursuers. When Brabham overtook him in the Parabolica curve he signalled to the Scot, who in fact had already guessed the problem, and half-turned in his cockpit to look at a rear wheel. A tyre was going flat.

Two laps later he rushed into the pits, where the wheel was quickly changed. But the clocks recorded

Jim Clark (Lotus 49) leading Denny Hulme (Brabham) in the 1967 Italian Grand Prix. Clark finished third, after a pit stop and running out of fuel when in the lead. Hulme blew his engine and retired, but went on to win the world championship

passed him before the end of the lap. But during the third lap of the 68-lap race, Clark was ahead. He had recovered from the excitement at the start, and with full tanks set new lap records on the second and third laps, only seven tenths of a second outside his best practice time.

Once in the lead, Clark settled down, keeping in front of the slipstreaming bunch which developed almost as usual in a Monza race. Hulme challenged briefly, but as the leaders swept into view to complete each lap, Hill was usually in second place.

that lap at over three minutes. Including slowing, Clark lost 1 minute 38 seconds, the equivalent of a lap of the track. He was just accelerating away when the leaders, Hulme, Brabham and Hill, shot past at 160 mph.

For a decade—since Fangio won that 1957 German Grand Prix—a pit stop in a Grand Prix had been a setback which virtually put a driver out of the running. The competition had become so keen that it was taken for granted that no driver could catch up once time and the initiative had been lost.

But Clark's character was strongly moulded in the hills of the Scottish borders. He could never accept defeat lightly. He had his share of what the Scots term 'dourness'. Perhaps the English would say implacable.

Graham Hill firmly led the Italian Grand Prix until his engine failed, and he trailed a cloud of smoke as he coasted to retire. This was the first year of the Cosworth engine in Formula 1; the next year it won the world championship, and has just gone on winning it

Although it hardly looked as if he was hurrying, Clark immediately began turning in laps in the 'one twenty-nines' again, and began to work his way through the field, albeit a lap behind the leaders. He restarted in 15th place, and within four laps had snatched back four places.

By lap 21 he had caught the leading group, and thus was exactly a lap in arrears. He overtook Hulme and Hill in one move, then on lap 28 the New Zealander slowed. He had tucked in behind Clark as he passed, but the strain had proved too much for his Repco engine, and he went out with a blown cylinder head. Brabham, too, began to trail, so that Hill opened a generous lead.

With a clear road ahead, Clark set a new lap record in 1 minute 28.5 seconds as he pounded on at a blistering pace, with Hill in his slipstream. The two Lotus drivers were leaving Brabham behind by two seconds a lap, and by lap 54, with 80 per

cent of the race run, were once again catching sight of him on the long straights.

So far it seemed that Clark was fighting only to reduce the margin by which he would finish behind the first placed drivers, but now inexorably he was making up a complete lap. The Team Lotus pair caught Rindt's Cooper-Maserati in fourth place, Hill lapping him, Clark making good most of that precious lost minute and a half. Hill passed Rindt, then just as Clark followed suit, the whole picture changed. Graham Hill's engine blew up in a puff of smoke, and the race leader was out.

Clark passed Surtees' Honda, and almost unbelievably was in second place again, behind Brabham and closing fast. He overtook to cheers which even he must have heard above the noise of his engine.

The Italians, to whom motor racing is an emotion-charged cult, were beside themselves with excitement. The tension of the pursuit had seemed unbearable, as they had realized that Clark might bring off the near-impossible feat of regaining the

Above: Italian spectators—the most emotional in motor racing.
Opposite: Jim Clark with Colin Chapman, Indianapolis, 1965

lead in a Grand Prix after losing a whole lap.

By lap 65, with three to go, Clark had managed to open a slight gap to Brabham. John Surtees had moved up, too, and he passed the Australian. The big electric scoreboard near the exit from the Parabolica, the last corner before the finish line, recorded 3.2 seonds covering the three cars after an hour and a half of racing. The margins were slender. On the next lap the margin was still 3.2 seconds—none of the drivers could make any impression.

On the last lap the Lotus faltered. Surtees and Brabham were past in a flash. They passed and re-passed in the final corner, Surtees inched ahead and out-fumbled Brabham to the flag.

Poor Clark. After his faultless and momentous drive, the Lotus came hiccupping round the Parabolica in third place. Its fuel pumps had failed to pick up the last three gallons in the tanks. The tumult and shouting of the near-riot crowd did not subside for two hours.

Jim Clark, the greatest driver ever. How we miss him.

Stirling Moss and Jackie Stewart were the two drivers who most influenced motor racing in the 1960s, for they personified the increasing trend towards professionalism. Drivers had become the focus of racing when the world championship shifted the emphasis away from the racing teams. At the same time, the cars were burdened with sometimes perplexing regulations, and some were to almost lose their identity under the weight of commercial advertising, as they had at Indianapolis much earlier. There, only enthusiasts could tell one car from another, while the drivers were household names. In Grand Prix racing, this march of events was inevitable, and even welcome to the survival of racing.

Moss and Stewart fully recognized the changing conditions of their times, which can partly be traced back to the social upheavals of the Second World War. The era of the professional sportsman arrived, in the sense that earning capacity was somehow related to talent. The days of the wealthy amateur were numbered in any case, and the scene

changed to the extent that the biggest compliment you could pay such amateurs as were left was to call them 'professional'.

In motor racing the seal was put on this revolution by drivers like Stirling Moss, who were simply so good that they were in demand. People who invested in racing cars, by design and development, or perhaps through the purchase of cars, wanted a return on their money in terms of publicity, certainly of success. If the only way to achieve this was to employ a driver of exceptional talent, provision must be made for him in the budget. There seemed little point in Rob Walker, for example, spending perhaps £50,000 on a racing team if for £60,000 he could buy a *successful* racing team capable of earning, say, £15,000 in a season.

In 1960 and 1961 Stirling Moss drove Walker's cars to win the Monaco Grand Prix. The record books state simply enough that the 1960 winner was Stirling Moss (Lotus Climax), in 2 hours 53 minutes 45.5 seconds, at 67.46 mph, while the fastest lap was put in by Bruce McLaren in a Cooper-Climax at 72.13 mph. In 1961 Stirling Moss won in a Lotus-Climax in 2 hours 45 minutes 50.1 seconds, at 70.70 mph; the fastest lap was shared by Moss and Ferrari driver Richie Ginther

at 72.05 mph, which represents a time round the streets of Monaco of 1 minute 36.3 seconds.

Those are the dry facts, but they are not enough – one also needs to know that the 1960 race was for cars with 2½ litre engines, and the 1961 race for cars with 1½ litre engines. Yet Moss' race average speed was nearly 3 mph *faster* in 1961. This was one of the most notable drives in a career that spanned 14 years of racing, and included victories in 16 Grands Prix.

Perhaps Moss' greatest victory came in the 1955 Mille Miglia, an epic event that used to be run for 1000 miles across Italy, on public roads in the tradition of the town-to-town races early in the Century. But in 1955 he had the might of Mercedes-Benz behind him. One of the qualities that distinguishes a great driver is the ability to win when things are going against him, to turn the tables on form.

In the Mille Miglia, the only major handicap was that Italian drivers knew the road intimately, and Moss could not possibly learn them in the way he learned circuits – you cannot come to know a thousand miles of road in a week, a fortnight, or even a month. It takes a lifetime, and even Mercedes-Benz were unable to stop the passage of time. So Moss took as a passenger Denis Jenkinson, who used pace notes to 'read' approaching corners to the driver; Moss thus became only the second foreign driver ever to win the Mille Miglia.

Stirling Moss' greatest sports car drive came in the 1955 Mille Miglia, when he was partnered by journalist Denis Jenkinson in a 300SLR Mercedes-Benz. The number represents their a.m. start time

At Monaco in 1961, there was even less in Moss' favour. He was driving for a small private team, which was equipped with a theoretically outclassed car. The 2½ litre formula had just given way to one restricting engine capacity to 1½ litres, and the Monaco Grand Prix was the first championship race to be run under the new regulations. The British constructors were not yet ready, for they had opposed the new rules. However, Britain's ascendancy in motor racing was not then sufficient for them to carry the day, and they were overruled, with the result that precious time was lost. Lotus had only just put their works cars together, and even if they had been able to sell one of their latest cars to Rob Walker for Stirling Moss to drive (their reluctance is understandable), they probably would not have been able to.

As the formula perpetuated the old Formula 2 some teams were fully prepared, notably Ferrari, who had two alternative engines ready for their rear-engined cars. These were a 65 degree V-6 which had been raced in Formula 2 in 1960, and a new 120 degree V-6. Producing 180–190 bhp, these gave the Ferrari drivers an advantage of 20–30 bhp over the drivers of British cars, even those with Mark 2 Coventry-Climax engines (which in any case few of the British teams had).

Stirling Moss did have one of these engines, but his car was an old Lotus 18, while the works team had new 21s for Clark and Ireland. The 18 had been the first rear-engined Lotus, originally appearing as a Formula Junior car; it had a tubular space frame, and while the works cars were fitted with ZF gearboxes, Moss' had a Colotti unit. Moss had gained for Lotus all their Grand Prix victories to this time, although Team Lotus looked certain to win a race 'on their own account' before long (and in fact were to do so, at Watkins Glen, before the end of the 1961 season).

On paper, Moss would be lucky to get into the first six at Monaco, behind the three Ferraris, the new low and slim Lotuses, while some of the other entries were by no means to be discounted.

The works Coopers had taken the world championships in 1959 and 1960, and their drivers at Monaco, Jack Brabham and Bruce McLaren, had the Mark 2 engines. So had the Yeoman Credit team Cooper driven by John Surtees, and the BRM driven by Graham Hill (BRM were waiting for their new V-8s to be built). There was also a Porsche team, but at this stage they were not a great threat.

The Ferrari team was full of confidence. An almost unknown driver, Giancarlo Baghetti, had just won the non-championship Syracuse Grand Prix for them, and at Monaco they had Phil Hill, a veteran, backed up by Richie Ginther and

Casino Square, Monaco. Richie Ginther and Stirling Moss pass the steps of the Hotel de Paris during their hard-fought 1961 race

Count Wolfgang Graf Berghe von Trips, one of the most gifted drivers in Europe.

Relative paper strengths of the teams notwithstanding, Rob Walker's dark blue Lotus was on pole position as the grid formed up for the start. Some of its side panelling was removed, for there was a hot afternoon's work ahead for Moss. Alongside him on the front row were Ginther and Clark, who shot away in the lead as the flag fell.

The green Lotus soon called at the pits, leaving Moss to chase the flying Ginther—up the hill, through Casino Square, down past the old Hotel

Mirabeau, round the Station Hairpin, and through the tunnel back onto the quayside, the blue Lotus was never out of the Ferrari driver's mirrors. Moss did not actually pass until lap 14, and he took Bonnier's Porsche with him. The Ferraris howled in pursuit, close and threatening, third, fourth and fifth.

One by one they gobbled up Bonnier, and the rest of the race consisted of a series of attacks on Moss by the Ferrari team. Ginther's were the most sustained. Lap after lap the pair were together round the tight course in the sunshine, the gap between them only fractions of seconds.

Practice laps are usually faster than race laps. They are done in ideal conditions, sometimes on an empty track, and represent a singular peak of performance when every gearchange and every turn of the wheel comes in the right sequence. But at Monaco in 1961, Moss and Ginther shaved off hundredths here, went closer to the limit there, and eventually were nearly three seconds a lap faster than they had been in practice. They got within a tenth of Bruce McLaren's $2\frac{1}{2}$ litre record, and the race record was smashed, raised from 67.46 mph to 70.70 mph, which was to remain unbeaten for two years. Moss won by less than four seconds. . . .

Jackie Stewart's affinity with Moss did not extend to failing in world championships, although it took him five years to win his first. Both drivers fostered the professional approach to racing, and both enjoyed leading races from the first lap (a characteristic shared by two of their immediate predecessors, Alberto Ascari and Jim Clark respectively). Unless their cars were off-colour or just not competitive, they would get ahead early. Even a theoretically uncompetitive car was not always a bar, as Moss showed at Monaco.

Stewart always claimed that early leads were best achieved by emotional control. He would have a personal count down before a race to diminish the excitement of the start, when drivers can get jumpy, and make mistakes.

After winning the 1969 World Drivers' Championship, he wrote, 'The major lesson (from 1968) . . . was the self-control that I had learned and its effect on my race performances. I had learned to start a race cleanly without emotional interference in my driving. This had been necessary partly because of the big sporting occasion that a Grand Prix is. A driver has an enormous responsibility to his team, the manufacturers of his car, his tyres and components, as well as himself and the people who have paid to watch. . . .

'I had started to learn the principle in 1968 although it showed itself more in 1969. It was something that I had to develop late in the season, in

Moss swinging Rob Walker's Lotus down to the sea front at Monaco in 1961

particular at Nürburgring and Watkins Glen and Mexico. Then I realised this was something that I had to cultivate deliberately. At first I just could not explain it and then it dawned on me that something was there, and there was a reason for it.

'It is nothing to do with natural ability, whatever that is. It is something that you first experience and then exploit. It was something that Jim Clark did not always have although he certainly brought it into play later in his career.

'I found that in the right frame of mind I could go out and hit a good lap time almost immediately through being in complete control of myself, through having arranged a mental build-up starting the day before.'

Stewart describes the beginning of the countdown, how he avoided parties or noisy groups of people the night before a race. He said he preferred to be with people with whom he did not constantly have to 'try'; people with whom he could relax.

'It starts when I go to bed. I have to get into neutral and fall asleep naturally. . . .' In the morning, he was still playing down the occasion, and '. . . instead of lying awake thinking about the race, or the weather, or who has been quicker than me in practice, I want a good book, or something to hold my interest. I realise it is an important day; I realise that I have a Grand Prix to do and I can become rather tense.'

He then used the analogy of a bouncy ball. Stewart is a bouncy sort of fellow. He is eager, sharp, and walks with a springy sort of step, on the balls of his feet. His words come quickly in his

Motor racing's first Superstar, Jackie Stewart. Persistent campaigner for safer motor racing, and one of the biggest money-earners in sport

Beginning of a fruitful partnership—Jackie Stewart in Ken Tyrrell's Formula 2 Matra at Goodwood. Stewart and Tyrrell later brought Matra into Formula 1; when they parted, Matra was the loser

clipped, characteristically Scottish manner.

On the morning of a race he had to deflate. The ball become less bouncy. 'If the ball remains too hard it has too much bounce and it is difficult to control, but if it is flat and unemotional, it will do nothing unexpected.'

He blunted his nervousness to try and set the pace of a race in the opening laps. The advantages of this were manifold.

First, it gives a driver a clear road until he catches up with the tail-enders again. This is important in the rain when the 'open-wheelers' trail a plume of spray. It means that there is nobody in the way; he can keep clear of nervous first lap drivers glancing off a kerb, or touching wheels with another car. When one of them spins and holds everyone up, it happens *behind* the leader.

Stewart was in this state of mind at the start of the German Grand Prix on the Nürburgring in 1968. This came at a critical point in the season, in a vital year of Stewart's career, and he was driving a new

car that still required vindication. So emotional control was all important.

In 1968, Jackie Stewart had left BRM. He had not won a Grand Prix since Monaco, 1966, just before his bad accident at Spa, and some people had already written him off as the Boy Wonder who had never made good. Stewart had briefly led in South Africa with the prototype Grand Prix Matra, and been sixth in the European opener, the Race of Champions at Brands Hatch. After an arm injury he missed both the Spanish and Monaco Grands Prix. With his wrist cased in a plastic sleeve he went to the Belgian Grand Prix at Spa. 'Everybody was a bit dubious about me driving, especially at Spa. Some of the press thought I had taken leave of my senses. "Here's Stewart going to drive in this Belgian Grand Prix where he had his accident a couple of years ago, and he's going to try and do it with one hand." '

Drive he did, and on that treacherous ribbon of road in the Ardennes he nearly won. A pit stop on the final lap dropped him to fourth.

At Zandvoort it rained. Jackie put on special new Dunlops, with rain grooves, and ran away with the

Stewart wins in the wet, at Zandvoort in 1968 when he gained
Matra's first Grand Prix victory. He used special grooved Dunlop tyres,
and was wearing a plastic sleeve to support his broken arm

race. 'It was the weather', said the sceptics,
'Dunlops are good in the wet.'

It rained again at Rouen in the French Grand
Prix, and Stewart was only third, so it couldn't
have been only the wet after all. Jo Siffert won at
Brands Hatch, where Stewart, his arm still giving
trouble, was sixth. So far in seven Grands Prix he
had been fast in practice, and fast in races, but he
had gained only one victory. If he really was as good
as he obviously thought he was, he needed to win
some more.

The eighth race was the European Grand Prix,
a courtesy title bestowed that year on the German
Grand Prix, at the most dramatic track in Europe,
the Nürburgring.

For three days the track high in the Eifel Mountains lay above the cloud base. For three days and
nights, the rain and fog were almost continuous.
Practice was intermittent. The road streamed with
water, and rain dripped incessantly on thousands
of spectators huddled miserably in tents amongst

the pines—as it has so often at the Nürburgring.

The order on the starting grid was not a reliable
guide to form, for this time it depended more on
conditions when drivers set their times than anything else. Stewart did not figure on the front two
rows, and his time was 50 seconds slower than
Jacky Ickx (Ferrari), winner at Rouen a month
before. If things remained as they were, Ickx was
due to lap Stewart well before the end of the 14 laps.

On race morning, the cloud lifted only long
enough for the course to be swept with rain. When
it closed in again, visibility was down to a matter of
yards, and was constantly changing, with rain, fog,
swirling mist, and more rain.

Officials debated, but eventually decided to start
the race. Ickx made a bad getaway, and half way
round the first lap Stewart lay second. Soon, the
big scoreboard looming out of the murk flashed
the news that the blue Matra was ahead. By the
time it completed the lap it was nine seconds in
front. A lap later, well under nine minutes for
Stewart, ten or more for everybody else, it was an
almost incredible 34 seconds ahead of Graham Hill
(Lotus). Then it was 47 seconds, and on lap 4 it

Left: Nebelmeister—master of the mists. Stewart races through the rain and mist at the Nürburgring in the most stirring drive of his career. Below: Veterans. Graham Hill (left) and Jack Brabham at Brands Hatch

Stewart got out of the car and talked to officials sheltering from the downpour, before Hill, Rindt, and Ickx burst into view.

Stewart's resounding win indicated that the Zandvoort result had been no fluke. He confirmed it by winning the United States Grand Prix, and coming to the final race of the season, still disputing the world championship with Graham Hill. He had to concede the title, but won it the following year.

The German race was the turning point. It

was 58 seconds. Stewart had pulled out nearly a minute on the next four cars. They in turn, passed within the space of nine seconds, close together, none able to break away in the welter of spray. They were Hill, Amon (Ferrari), Rindt (Brabham), and Ickx (Ferrari). Then came another gap of over a minute to Brabham and Hulme.

At twelve laps, Stewart was two minutes ahead. Rain still swept the course, the gloom deepened in the valleys between the trees. At the end of the race, the Matra took a sodden chequered flag. Stewart drove past, through the South Curve, and back up the long straight behind the pits, almost a mile. He turned, stopped, and switched off the engine. The patter of rain on a sea of umbrellas broke the sudden hush. His pursuers were not within earshot.

emphasised that Jackie Stewart was one of the best drivers of his time. And it ended the interruption to his success—an interruption which had also begun on a rain-soaked track, at Spa more than two years earlier.

If the criterion of greatness in a racing driver is success in the face of adversity, then Graham Hill qualifies on this basis alone as a great racing driver. In the same way that Hill won five Monaco Grands Prix, on the circuit that probably makes the greatest demands of precision and skill on a racing driver, so he conquered the effects of an accident that might have concluded many another driver's career.

Hill won the Monaco Grand Prix for the first

time in 1963. The previous year he had been world champion, and given BRM their first manufacturers' cup. Clark and Lotus were beaten into second place. The 1963 season was to see the tables turned; it was the year Clark won a record seven Grands Prix in a season. But on the last week of May there was still not much to choose between the tall, angular Londoner with his dark green V-8 BRM, and the small, wiry Scotsman and the green and yellow Lotus with its Coventry-Climax V-8.

They were together on the front row of the grid. Clark had the edge on speed, but his car failed, and Graham Hill won at 72.42 mph, with his team-mate Richie Ginther second.

The following year, 1964, Graham Hill won again. When leading, Clark had to make a pit stop as the rear anti-roll bar of his Lotus came loose. Hill dealt with stiff opposition from Jack Brabham and Dan Gurney, particularly, to once again head Richie Ginther past the flag, giving the BRM team a one-two record for two successive years.

The next year, 1965, Graham Hill won yet again. Once more, BRM were well placed, for third place was taken by their newest recruit, Jackie Stewart, who was to interrupt Hill's run of success at Monaco. Hill had scored the hat trick, and in 1966 the 1965 positions were reversed: Stewart was first, Hill was third.

By 1967 the 3 litre cars were competing in earnest. Hill was now driving for Team Lotus, who were waiting for the Ford-Cosworth engine, and as a stand-in were using a 2 litre version of the BRM V-8, with which Hill had raced since 1962. The best he could manage with this litre handicap at Monaco was a courageous second place to Denny Hulme, who drove a Brabham-Repco.

Graham Hill's record at Monaco was achieved principally through discipline. This circuit demands two qualities above all of a driver. He needs to be able to place a car accurately throughout 80 laps (100 until 1968), avoiding the kerbs, walls, culverts and other trackside obstacles that make the course a slalom-like test of precise driving. He needs to be able to drive smoothly, despite more gearchanges, heavy braking, sharp corners, gradient and camber changes per mile than any other circuit. Snatched gear changes, abrupt use of the clutch and heavy braking mean that a car is strained more at Monaco than any other circuit, and this puts a premium on strictly disciplined driving.

Much of the appeal of motor racing is its variety, and many qualities other than sheer speed are needed to win races. At Monaco, Hill has demonstrated the importance of an ability to concentrate, and triumph over an exquisite test for man and machine.

In 1968, with three Monaco Grands Prix in his

Above: Graham Hill on his way to his first Monaco Grand Prix victory, with the BRM in 1963. The great Jim Clark, who never achieved his ambition of a Monaco win, follows him down to the chicane. Right: Hill in the 'semi-wedge' Lotus 49 during his 1968 winning drive

trophy room, Hill had to take a new dimension into account. Team Lotus had just lost Jim Clark, and was in a state of shock over the death of the man around whose driving the team had virtually been built.

They still had the 49, and Graham Hill had driven it to win at the new Jarama track in Spain. At Monaco it had a new wedge-shaped body, designed to provide an aerodynamic downthrust to help gain extra traction, especially grip in corners. With it Hill notched up a fourth great Monaco win, in another exhibition of concentrated skill at the wheel – throughout much of the race Richard Attwood's BRM was only a few lengths away in pursuit.

In 1969 Hill triumphed yet again at Monaco, and again in conditions of adversity. Two weeks earlier,

on the Montjuich circuit at Barcelona, Hill and his new Lotus team mate Jochen Rindt both had catastrophic 'wing' failures, and crashed on the fastest part of the course. Hill pulled Rindt from the wreck of his car. At Monaco the FIA banned wings, suddenly depriving the cars of part of their cornering power.

Nevertheless, Hill took the chequered flag yet again, to gain his fifth Monaco victory.

This was not the last time that Graham Hill was to show plain courage in a racing car. That same year he crashed in the Grand Prix of the United States, his Lotus doing a terrifying cartwheel in the Loop Chute at Watkins Glen when a tyre failed. Hill broke both legs, and was in hospital for the rest of the year. When he came out, his walk had changed from a jaunty, cowboy-style lope to a halting limp.

For months more, he avoided lifts, preferring to walk upstairs and exercise his shattered limbs. Friends took him on one side and tried to persuade him to hang up his helmet. It seemed time he

Left: Graham Hill's accident at Barcelona. The Lotus crested the rise to the left of the top photograph, and the rear wing broke, depriving the wheels of their grip on the road. It bounced across the circuit to the opposite side of the road, where Hill climbed out. A few laps later Rindt's Lotus suffered the same failure, and was destroyed in a similar accident.
Below: After his serious accident at Watkins Glen later in the same year, Hill returned to racing early in 1970, in the South African Grand Prix

retired. But with Graham Hill, things were not as easy as that.

'I enjoy motor racing,' he said. 'I want to go on doing it. It is very nice of people to show such concern about me, and I always thank them very much, but I don't want to give it up.'

His target was the South African Grand Prix of 1970. He had joined the Rob Walker team. His doctors advised him against getting back into a racing car; another accident like that in America would have been disastrous, yet at 41 years of age, he risked it. Failure would have been understandable, yet to Hill it was unthinkable. It was not a private struggle. Hill drove painfully in the South African Grand Prix under the gaze not only of thousands of spectators, but with the Press of the world looking on and waiting—sympathetically—but still waiting for him to give in.

He did not give in. He went the distance and finished sixth.

He had to wait for another year before winning a major race, and he had to change to a Brabham to do it, but the crowd at Silverstone the following spring that saw Graham Hill winning the 1971 International Trophy, showed their appreciation of a performance that marked out the twice world champion as one of the most popular, and one of the bravest drivers ever to sit behind the wheel of a racing car.

Above: John Surtees (Surtees-Ford) in the Karussel at Nürburgring. Right: beside the harbour, Monaco 1971. Pedro Rodriguez (Yardley BRM) leads Ronnie Peterson (STP March), Denny Hulme (Gulf McLaren) and Chris Amon (Matra-Simca) in pursuit of race-leader Jackie Stewart

World Championship

By the end of 1971, the World Drivers' Championship had been in existence for 22 years. Nearly two hundred Grand Prix races (to be precise, one hundred and ninety eight) had been contested by 259 drivers, of whom just under half never reached leading places.

The total of races has varied from as few as six in 1950, when the championship was instituted, to 13 in 1970, when the title was awarded posthumously to Jochen Rindt.

Three drivers, Jim Clark, Juan Manuel Fangio and Jackie Stewart together won 66 of the races; exactly one-third. Clark was the highest scorer with 25 victories, Fangio won two-fifths of his 58 races, most world championships, five in all, and he also scored at the fastest rate, averaging 4.52 championship points for every race he started.

Graham Hill competed in more races than any other driver, a total of 135 times, won the highest total of championship points (289), and although

he only won 14 championship races he was placed on 36 occasions, which constituted another record. Only 35 drivers scored outright wins, and Jim Clark set more fastest laps than anyone else.

The scoring system changed from time to time, one of its vagaries making Stirling Moss the unluckiest driver over the years. He won 16 races, by far the highest of any driver who never won a world championship. The great Italian Alberto Ascari won two titles with 13 victories.

Jim Clark held the record for the largest number of victories in a single season, seven in 1963, and he is the only driver in the leading half dozen to have scored all his wins, indeed driven all his Grands Prix, in only one make of car, Lotus.

The most famous dispute in the totals of Grand Prix wins concerns Fangio. Between 1950 and 1957,

a driver whose car dropped out of a race could take over another, and inherit the race position of its driver, his team-mate; championship points were thus awarded jointly. Fangio did this on two occasions and won, and there has been controversy ever since about whether these two wins ought to be credited separately or counted as 'half-wins' thereby reducing his most-often quoted total of 24 to 23. Thus, Moss would only count $15\frac{1}{2}$ for the same reason, and Tony Brooks $5\frac{1}{2}$. But it brings into the tables Luigi Fagioli, and Luigi Musso, both with 'half-wins', being the drivers whose cars Fangio took over (Moss and Brooks shared the winning Vanwall in the 1957 British Grand Prix at Aintree).

The countries with most championships are Argentina with five, by virtue of the singular Fangio, then England with four, and Scotland with four. Italian and Australian drivers have each won the title three times, and drivers from the United States, Austria, and New Zealand have taken it once each.

By the end of the period, out of the 12 title winners, only four were still racing. Three were living in retirement from the track, and five were

Opposite: Phil Hill, only American ever to win the world championship, during the 1961 German Grand Prix.
Below: The two great Scottish champions racing together. Jackie Stewart (BRM) just ahead of Jim Clark (Lotus) in the 1967 Australian Grand Prix, a race in the Tasman Series, which Clark won

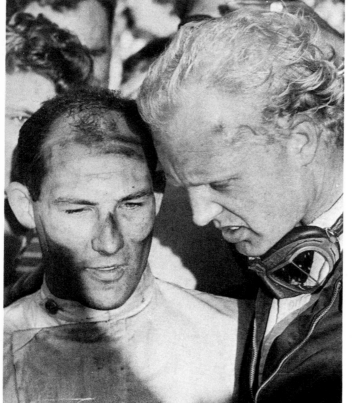

dead. All died at the wheels of cars, but only one during a race. Jim Clark was killed at Hockenheim in April, 1968 during a relatively unimportant Formula 2 event. Alberto Ascari was enjoying a friend's sports car in a private trial at Monza, when he crashed and was killed. Jochen Rindt, with the championship almost in his grasp, died in his Lotus 72 during practice for the 1970 Italian Grand Prix at almost the same spot. Mike Hawthorn was driving his Jaguar on the Guildford by-pass not far from his home in 1958, when he crashed and was fatally injured. He had won the championship, and retired from racing. Giuseppe Farina was killed in a road accident in France in 1966.

Of the former Grand Prix winners, fourteen were dead by 1971, twelve had retired, and eleven were still racing. Of the dead only three, Peter Collins, Count Wolfgang Graf Berghe von Trips and Lorenzo Bandini had died while taking part in Grand Prix races. Only Stirling Moss had retired through injury, and all of the survivors, with the exception of Froilan Gonzalez were still actively connected with motor racing.

When the Championship was introduced the immediate post-war Formula was about to end. This was the $1\frac{1}{2}$ litre supercharged/$4\frac{1}{2}$ litres unsupercharged arrangement which had served so well since 1947. It had been due to expire in 1953, but in fact ended prematurely. The big unsupercharged Ferraris had forced Alfa Romeo to beat a hurried retreat into retirement, for their supercharged Type 158/159 was at the end of its useful life. The danger of Ferrari walk-overs was only too obvious, because clearly BRM were not in a position to offer opposition, and nobody else was in much shape to do so either. Race organisers selected something that would continue to bring in the crowds.

So the 1952 and 1953 Championship races were held to Formula 2 rules, which specified a maximum capacity of 2 litres unsupercharged, or 500 cc with

Top: Giuseppe Farina, the first world champion driver, in 1950. Coached by Nuvolari, he began racing in the 1930s, and retired in 1955; five years later he died in a road accident.
Left: Stirling Moss, second in the world championship four years in a row, three times to Fangio, and once to Mike Hawthorn, winner in 1958.
Opposite: significant winning combinations. Jack Brabham shows his characteristic style in a Cooper-Climax, the marque that twice won the constructor's championship, in 1960 (top) and in a Repco-Brabham in the 1966 French Grand Prix, when he became the first driver to win a championship race in a car bearing his own name

Left: a very determined Jack Brabham cornering his Cooper-Alta in his first race in England, at the Goodwood Easter Meeting in 1955, and fourteen years later in a Brabham-Ford with 'biplane' aerofoils.
Above: Graham Hill airborne in a BRM at the Nürburgring

superchargers. The lower limit was an impractical one, and no cars of this size ever raced.

From 1954 to 1960, the maximum capacity of $2\frac{1}{2}$ litres was used by all the competing cars, even though 750 cc supercharged designs were technically admissible. An important alteration to the rules came in 1958, when 100–130 octane 'pump' fuel was introduced at the behest of the oil companies who were, as always, deeply involved in the financial structure of the sport. They wanted to claim in their advertising that races had been won on their standard fuel, and not the exotic mixtures that had been employed for many years. It was a sensible rule; it kept racing from becoming too esoteric, but it did mean that cars were rather more liable to catch fire in an accident.

In 1961 the rules were changed again. The 1957–60 Formula 2 was 'promoted', and became the

Formula 1 until 1965. Engine capacity was limited to $1\frac{1}{2}$ litres, and superchargers were banned. A minimum weight of 450 Kg was introduced in the belief that without the need to design cars as light as possible, they would be made strong. 'Pump' fuel was still compulsory, and the cars had to be equipped with self-starters. Replenishment of oil was forbidden.

The self-starter rule and the oil filling ban were introduced with an eye to safety, which was becoming an important consideration. The Le Mans disaster was still fresh in the mind of the Federation International de l'Automobile when it framed the rules, and they did not wish governments to ban the sport wholesale in the emotional aftermath. Safety became respectable, and nonsensical braying that motor racing ought to remain dangerous, or lose its 'character', began to sound outmoded.

Unfortunately, the self-starter rule had a side-effect. It meant that cars had to carry batteries, which were a source of sparks following an accident, and yet another fire risk. The oil rule was accepted to prevent leaky cars continuing to race, and laying a carpet of the stuff all round a circuit every time they refilled the sump.

The $1\frac{1}{2}$ litre Formula did not produce spectacular cars. But it did produce some very close racing, big fields of well-matched cars, and a huge upsurge of

public interest. The changeover to mid-engined cars was completed, and although 240 horse power may not have taxed drivers' courage, it taxed their skill to make the most of what power the engines did give. It also stimulated chassis design. Road holding was at a premium because with the numbers of proprietary engines in use, and the similarity of power outputs even amongst rival cars, meant that it was the only major area where an advantage could be gained.

In 1966 engine capacity was raised to 3 litres, and gradually more safety measures were also instituted, like roll-over bars behind the cockpits, to prevent drivers being trapped in overturned cars. Fire extinguishers, bag-type fuel tanks, and other features became mandatory. Wider tyres and improvements in roadholding complemented increases in power to between 400 and 450 bhp, although most engines in the first year of the Formula were hard pressed to show more than 375 bhp with any reliability.

Race distances diminished over the years: 300 kilometres or three hours until 1957, then between 300 and 500 kilometres *and* two hours between 1958 and 1965, down to between 300 and 400 kilometres.

Throughout the period, the success of the Championship was assured by increased Press and television coverage. The reasons for this have always been hotly debated, but it seems beyond doubt that the increasingly important role played by drivers in motor racing caught the public imagination. Fangio, Moss, Clark, and Stewart became popular heroes in a way that their pre-war counterparts never did—in those days it was principally countries and teams that had raced against one another.

The ascendancy of individuals was probably an expression of the improved status of the individual during the years after the war. Motor racing was reflecting social change as much as anything else. It was a trend that drivers, and in time trade sponsors, exploited to provide sources of income, and the earnings of drivers like Stewart, Hulme, Rindt, and others in the late 1960s came into line with professionals in other sports like golf, soccer, and even that rather gory Spanish branch of show-business with which motor racing is so often quite erroneously equated, bull-fighting.

Motor racing in the period of the World Drivers' Championship became more democratic in the sense that almost anyone, given the will, could join in, although there is no doubt that personal wealth helped many a driver to gain entry to the sport. Yet dole-queue to riches stories were by no means exceptional. Fangio was not wealthy in his early days and Graham Hill was probably the most famous example of a former mechanic who later made the grade; they, and others, can attribute the accumulation of considerable fortunes chiefly to the institution in 1950 of the most important and prestigious of all the FIA Championships.

Corners

If any group of drivers was asked to name the toughest corners in racing, the answers would be individual, and vary widly. Nominations in 1960 and 1970, and if it comes to it in 1980, would be different again, not so much of tracks that came and went, but because cars changed. Bends that might have been 'flat' in the 1950s with 250 horse power engines needed more care in the 1960s, and perhaps a dab on the brakes by the 1970s. Other corners which might have been rated 'difficult' in earlier decades may have become relatively easy, because of progress in tyre and suspension design.

Car have become wider, and this has affected the lines drivers take through corners. The change to mid-engined cars meant that the characteristics of some corners altered, while the move towards reclining driving positions completely altered drivers' views of the road–an apex, or 'clipping point', previously used as an aiming mark disappeared over the brow of a hill from such a low eye level. Bends have become 'blind', and the whole art of race driving more difficult. Nuvolari's generation, used to high cockpits with commanding views of the road, could hardly have envisaged a wide-tyred racing car with a hammock-style driving position, let alone the capability of cornering 'on rails', with drivers aiming at points which they could not see on the edges of roads.

Speed alone does not make corners difficult. Drivers have different criteria, and it depends on what is meant by difficult, or tough, or great. A concensus of opinion among Grand Prix and sports car drivers, and the racing journalists and photographers who observe them at close quarters, produced many answers, but at least some agreement on the severity of some corners. In a few cases, single corners were not specified. For example, it was suggested that virtually any corner on the great Madonie circuit over which the Targa Florio is run could be considered difficult; Daytona was singled out simply for sheer speed through its

Paddock Bend, Brands Hatch. **Above:** two Porsche 917s in the 1970 BOAC 1000 km splash gingerly down the hill; the second is approaching the apex, which the driver could not see from the approach. **Right,** quick work by marshals rescued Andrea de Adamich from his crashed and burning Ferrari at Paddock

banked turns; the series of sharp corners on the downhill section of the circuit in Barcelona's Montjuich Park were reckoned to be one of the best and most testing sequences in racing; drivers thought Clermont-Ferrand exciting, without singling out particular corners.

Brands Hatch

Clearways, Paddock and Bottom Bend are the most testing corners on the Kent circuit, but at least one driver thinks that Brands is such a mess that it does not deserve nomination for anything.

Clearways, the last corner before the start/finish line, is a 120 degree bend with an increasing radius, which in plan looks straightforward. But the ground drops away throughout most of its length, the camber is towards the outside, and the surface is patchy. There is little agreement on its 'standard of difficulty', for drivers can brake into it on a straight, and more than one line can safely be taken through it.

Paddock and Bottom Bends are considered much more demanding. Paddock in particular is fast, but the ground drops away very sharply, the approach on a slight bend is difficult and the corner is invisible from the braking area. Drivers felt that a mistake on the approach to Paddock could be serious, and once committed to a line there is only one way through.

Spa-Francorchamps

This was for many years the fastest road circuit in the world, and featured two outstanding high-speed corners, Burnenville and the Masta 'kink'.

Burnenville was not a single corner, but a series of downhill right-handers which in a little over half a mile turned the circuit through 180 degrees. These were taken nearly 'flat'–with the throttle wide open–and in common with many of the world's most difficult corners, there was only one way round, one path or line which allowed Burnenville to be taken in one smooth sweep at high speed. A deviation of a few feet would certainly result in loss of time, and perhaps an accident.

Part of Burnenville's character was lost when an artificial chicane was introduced at Malmédy, to slow the exit and thus the whole corner, after several drivers had left the road in the 1966 Belgian Grand Prix.

Another 'knife edge' corner was the kink in the middle of the famous Masta straight. Here drivers had to snake, slalom-style, through a shallow 'S'

Contrasting corners. Left: an Alfa Romeo T33-3 in a tight Sicilian village street during the 1971 Targa Florio. Above: Burnenville, Spa, with sports cars in another championship event, the 1000 km, swinging through a corner at the other end of the speed range. Below: the 1971 Indianapolis pace lap in Turn 1—this ended disastrously when the pace car overshot the pits and injured several photographers

between buildings and down a slight incline—at perhaps 185 mph, judgment had to be precise. Very few drivers could take the Masta kink in a Grand Prix car, or a big sports car, without momentarily lifting off the throttle.

Indianapolis
In theory, all four corners on the famous oval track are identical but to drivers they are all different. To begin with, two are approached by only short straights, two by long straights, so that only diagonally opposite pairs are strictly comparable. Turn 1 is considered more difficult than Turn 3, largely because the approach—at around 200 mph—seems bumpier.

Braking is critical at Indianapolis, and entry to the turns important. The choice of braking point dictates the whole corner, and in turn the speed down the next straight. Pedal pressure has to be exactly right, and a light touch is vital, so that a car does not 'nose-dive'—this devours time, as the car has to adjust to its proper ride-height.

With braking so important, anything else imposed on a driver's mind in the braking area distracts, and Turn 1 has distractions. The shadow of the grandstand can affect judgment, a driver will

still be digesting information from a pit board, and he must watch for cars leaving the pit road. Demands on concentration add up to make Turn 1 at Indianapolis a difficult corner.

Kyalami

Crowthorne and Jukskei at this South African circuit were both mentioned, the former because it comes at the end of a long straight and could be tricky in the opening laps of a race when cars are still closely bunched, the latter because it is fast—around 160 mph—and is a point where a good driver can gain an advantage.

Monaco

In its pre-1972 form the chicane at Monaco was unanimously agreed to be one of the outstanding corners in motor racing. On a circuit with three hairpins, four 90 degree corners and two 45 degree bends, any third or fourth gear corner is fast.

The chicane serves to shift the track from the road leading away from the tunnel onto the parallel quayside. After Lorenzo Bandini's fatal accident in 1967 it was moved a few feet closer to the Tabac

Corner, and when the pits were moved to the quayside in 1972 it was moved as near to the Tabac as possible, where it had been arranged in the mid-1930s.

Approached down a ramp from the tunnel, and with a sheer rock face on the right, the Chicane was forbidding. In its high-speed swerve wheels brushed the wooden balustrade, and it called for great precision and delicacy. It was on one of the fastest parts of the circuit, and a point where a smooth, careful driver could gain an advantage.

Monza

The Italian autodrome, some ten miles outside Milan, is one of the traditional Grand Prix circuits, and has been in use since 1922. It is also one of the fastest circuits, with a lap speed of over 150 mph, but its most interesting corner is its slowest, the Parabolica—some of the fastest drivers feel that they alone make the best use of it.

The Parabolica is part of the old road circuit, returning cars from the back leg of the 3.57 mile track to the long fast straight past the pits. As the Curvetta, it was once a slightly banked perfect semicircle, but when the high-speed track was built in 1955 it was re-aligned as an almost level bend with an ever-widening radius (96.39 metres through the first 100 degrees, steadily increasing for the remaining 80 degrees). The idea was that when the high-speed track and road circuit were used in conjunction, two streams of cars would converge smoothly.

The chicane, Monaco, scene of many accidents, which were seldom serious until Lorenzo Bandini's in 1967. Left: Nuvolari races past the wreckage of Farina's Alfa Romeo and von Brauchitsch' Mercedes-Benz in 1936. Below: 3 litre cars swing through in a blare of sound in 1967. Right, top: Varied cars entering the Parabolica at Monza—a Porsche 917 squeezes between a Porsche touring car and an Alfa Romeo in the leading trio. Right, Dusk at Le Mans. The sprint race of the first hours is over. Ahead lies a night's drive.

The high-speed track was rarely used, so the original purpose of the re-alignment was seldom fulfilled. The Parabolica is not in itself difficult, but at high speeds it presents a challenge of a slow entry and fast exit—cars reach the braking area on the Rettilineo Centrale straight at between 180 and 200 mph.

Drivers change into second or third gear—this depending largely on the fuel load—and then try to keep 'in the groove' all the way round. The surface of the Parabolica outside the line tends to be covered in loose gravel, and extremely slippery. So a driver has to keep his line, and hit the apex exactly, in order to achieve a good exit, and thus gain speed as quickly as possible for the long, decisive straight—a slow exit from this corner can mean the loss of 50 yards and losing the 'tow' of the leader's slipstream has put many a driver out of the running here.

Unhappily, the entry to the Parabolica has a bad accident record. Jochen Rindt died here, and so did Count Graf Berghe von Trips in 1961, together with 11 spectators. It has had its share of drama, too. Graham Hill lost the 1965 Grand Prix to Stewart in the Parabolica, and Brabham the 1967 race to Surtees, both of them because of loose gravel at the edge of the road. Rindt and Beltoise lost in 1969 to Stewart, and in 1971 Gethin gained the narrowest of margins over a slipstreaming quartet.

Mosport

Another corner where the right line and a loose surface at the edge of the road are important factors in Turn 1 at Mosport. This is a long downhill left-hander, off-camber and with the apex out of sight over a crest. So there is a single ideal line, and the successful drivers keep strictly to the groove.

Nürburgring

This circuit is most often nominated the world's toughest by drivers and photographers. While spectators tend to favour the Karussel, or the bumps at Brunnchen where cars used to leap clear of the track for several yards, drivers think of whole stretches, in particular the series of bends down to Adenau Bridge, or the length between the Karussel and Schwalbenschwanz.

The Karussel is one of the most famous corners in racing. It comes between the 13th and 14th kilometre posts on the 14.2 mile track, after a long winding climb from Kesselchen. It turns almost full circle, and was originally built with a concreted drainage ditch on the inside. Traditionally, Caracciola's riding mechanic is credited with discovering its time-saving value as a lower banking, in 1929, shortly after the circuit was built.

It makes heavy demands on cars and men. Centrifugal force rams the cars down on their springs, onto the rubber bump stops, habitually set at the 'Ring for this corner alone, to prevent the underside of a car scraping the road. The driver is pressed down in his seat, and the steering kicks back in his hands, as the car reacts like an animal being made to

Monza, 1971—line astern, line abreast. Recent Italian Grands Prix have been extremely close-fought, as drivers alternately slipstream or jostle for the lead. Peterson (March), Stewart (Tyrrell), Siffert (BRM) and Regazzoni (Ferrari) lead this 1971 Grand Prix nose to tail group; Peterson, Cevert (Tyrrell), Hailwood (Surtees) and Siffert race side by side

Above: the Karussel in its 1971 form, with a Lotus 72 down in the 'ditch', where 'g' loadings press cars down on their springs and teams add special bump rubbers to suspension.
Below: Woodcote, with cars streaming through at 140 mph. Concrete road on left leads to the pits

perform a strenuous and most unnatural trick.

This has never been a corner where drivers have been able to make up much time. From the moment of entry, most of it remained out of sight, even before the days of reclining positions. It very literally has to be taken 'in the groove', and once committed there is little chance for talent to improve matters. Accurate braking is essential, and a good exit important, in preparation for the difficult sequence of corners which follows.

Oulton Park

This road circuit has one of the most exciting corners in England, Lodge, which has an out-of-sight apex and a steep downhill exit, taking the weight off the wheels at the critical point where grip is most needed.

Silverstone

Jackie Stewart describes Woodcote as one of the most difficult corners in the world, for its appearance belies its nature and at 130 mph it calls for a high degree of skill. It is a very long corner, taking cars onto the straight past the pits. Starting grids form up on it, and races are lost and won on it

Cars reach their highest speeds at two points on the three mile Silverstone track, down Hangar straight and on the approach to Woodcote. On the return leg, drivers accelerate out of Club and through the slight Abbey Bend left-hander, so that under the road bridge over the approaches to Woodcote a Grand Prix car is travelling at between 165 and 175 mph.

At that speed long waves on the track surface become sharp bumps, and these make it difficult to keep to the right path; if Woodcote is to be taken fast, smoothly and safely, there is only one line. The fastest drivers just brush their brakes on the way in—not too hard or the critical front to rear balance is upset—and then apply power early and progressively all the way through the corner. Flat, wide, and needing much more skill than might be imagined, Woodcote epitomises Silverstone.

Artificial courses can be fine, safe and exciting venues for road races. But possibly they are being designed a little too carefully, and very flat sites have been chosen for some. Interestingly, when drivers are asked to name challenging corners, they do not nominate any at tracks like the splendid Paul Ricard circuit in France, or the Ontario Motor Speedway in California. They talk about the long-established traditional circuits, like Monaco or the Nüburgring, tracks with unplanned hazards, irregularities and difficulties that test their skill.

Opposite, top: Ferrari's fourth win in as many races in their triumphant 1972 sports car season came at Brands Hatch in the BOAC 1000 km. Two of the team's 312Ps, driven by Ickx and Regazzoni, sweep past John Bamford's 2 litre Chevron up the approach to the Druids hairpin. Left: Vast crowds waiting for the start of the 1971 24-hour race for touring cars on the classic Spa-Francorchamps circuit in the Ardennes. Above: Spectators crowd a natural grandstand at the Osterreichring during the 1970 Austrian Grand Prix. Giunti (Ferrari) leads Rindt (Lotus) and Brabham (Brabham) through the corner on a wide line

Sports Car Racing

One event, the Le Mans 24 Hour Race, has so strongly influenced all that has ever happened in sports car racing that the two are practically synonymous. Without in the least denying the importance of the world sports car championship, the status of races at Daytona and Sebring, the long-established Targa Florio, the 1 000 Kilometre races at the Nürburgring, Spa, Brands Hatch, Monza and Buenos Aires, or the sometimes fragile relationship between Le Mans and the rest of the motor sporting world, the French 24-hour race

occupies a unique place in the history of four-wheeled motor sport. Le Mans is to road racing what the Monte Carlo Rally is to rallies, the Indianapolis 500 to track racing, Wimbledon to tennis, the British Open Championship to golf or the Marathon to running.

It is not the most testing sports car race, nor the oldest. It is not the fastest, nor necessarily the most difficult. Its quality has varied over the years, and it has often seemed to be in decline. It is not the safest, nor the most dangerous, although it holds the doubtful distinction of having witnessed the worst single disaster in the whole history of the sport. The organisers have been accused—not without

Le Mans start. Traditional opening for this sports car classic last used in 1969, when seat belts ruled it out. The cars lined up in echelon in 1970, then in 1971 a rolling start was used

Left: the American Stutz that so nearly won the 1928 Le Mans 24-hour Race leads a Bentley past the pits. Right: a streamlined car in 1929, in the old Pontlieue hairpin which was abandoned after that year's race. This Tracta, later to retire, is followed by the Clement-Chassagne Bentley which finished fourth behind three similar cars

reason – of meanness. They have introduced arbitrary regulations without warning to suit their own ends. They are commercially minded without a doubt, and just as the World Cup does not reflect all of soccer, or the Olympic Games all of athletics, so Le Mans does not reflect all of two-seater, or sports car, racing.

This is a world of which Can-Am is, or ought to be, the summit. Yet Le Mans, with its singular history virtually unbroken except by the Second World War, has become the apotheosis of the racing sports car.

Regulations at Le Mans, and in this category of motor racing as a whole, have often been contentious affairs. When the race was started in 1923, it

seemed fairly straightforward to insist upon catalogued models. They had to be equipped with wings, lights, hood, horn and mirrors, and kits of tools and spares had to be carried on the car. The race was to be a test of a car's suitability as a practical touring car, as well as a competition. A declaration that at least 30 similar models had been sold, or were about to be, was obligatory.

All cars over 1100 cc had to have four seats, but by 1930 this rule was relaxed to 1½ litres, and by 1937, even this had been changed to a minimum of two comfortable seats. Regulations like this have always been a nuisance. What is a 'comfortable' seat? To whom did it have to be comfortable? A slip of a girl, or the portly president of the Automobile Club de l'Ouest?

Ballast equivalent to passengers had to be carried at first, and in the early races weather equipment had to be demonstrated. This rule too was later relaxed, and then re-imposed during the 1950s, but by then Le Mans competitors had become so accustomed to idiosyncratic laws that it was laughed off the following season.

Minimum distances before refuelling were prescribed, with the object of preventing the entry of

Ferraris in the Esses in 1961, during a period when the Italian marque ruled supreme at Le Mans. Olivier Gendebien in the winning car which he shared with Phil Hill leading Richie Ginther in an outwardly very similar, but rear-engined, Ferrari

Classic sports cars. Opposite: Ron Flockhart in the winning Ecurie Ecosse Jaguar D-type rounding Mulsanne in 1957, on his way to the second Scottish victory at Le Mans, and the fifth and final victory for Jaguar in this race. Opposite, below: Stirling Moss in an Aston Martin DBR1 at Goodwood in 1958.
Below: A Ford GT40 of the Gulf-backed John Wyer team at Le Mans. Ford's string of victories in the 24-hour race between 1966 and 1969 culminated when Jacky Ickx and Jack Oliver co-drove this car to dramatically win from the Porsche driven by Herrman and Larrousse

freakish cars. How effective they have been is debatable.

After the war, production figures were relaxed, and then raised to 100 cars. Prototypes were introduced, qualifying as cars which the manufacturers *intended* to put into production.

Following the 1955 tragedy, Le Mans fell into line with other big sports car events until the GT classification was introduced a few years later in an attempt to do away with machines that were more like two seat racing cars than sports cars. The famous 'spirit of the regulations' controversy came about when the governing Automobile Club de l'Ouest tried to make up its own mind about what was a legitimate sports car and what manifestly was not. The club's successive failures to define catalogued sports cars without reducing the event to a race for touring cars, reflected the dilemma of this branch of racing. On the one hand there were two seat racing cars, and on the other, touring cars. Somewhere in between, within a hotch-potch of unwieldy, contentious regulations, came racing machines called sports cars.

The tragic year of 1955 marks a watershed in the history of the sports racing car. Up till then, the cars did by and large qualify in the original spirit of Le Mans. They were generally honestly catalogued, and for the most part resembled road cars, available to the public. They were identifiable as belonging to a make which could be seen in dealers' showrooms.

In 1953 for example, the Jaguar XK120Cs which came first, second and fourth had substantially the same 3.4 litre engine as those in the production saloon and XK sports cars. The C-Type itself was a catalogued model. The Cunninghams which came third, seventh and tenth were in limited production, albeit at a very high price indeed, but the 4.1 litre Ferrari which came fifth was by no means cheap either. The sixth-placed

Above: the Chaparral 2F was the first modern racing car to use a practical aerofoil, appearing with it at Bridgehampton in 1966. Later it won sports car championship events in Europe, here the 1967 BOAC 500 at Brands Hatch'
Opposite, top: Gulf Porsche team mates Siffert and Rodriguez racing each other very closely in the 1970 Spa 1000 km—their cars are touching at about 120 mph in Tertre Rouge. Below: Pit stop. The Penske Ferrari 512M driven by Donohue and Hobbs at Daytona in 1971

Gordini was not in series production, but it was not an extravagant 'one-off', and even the Talbot which was placed eighth and was an old Grand Prix car equipped with bodywork and lights was in the best traditions of motor racing, going back to the days of the Type 35 Bugatti. Another C-Type Jaguar was ninth and eleventh was a Nash-Healey based firmly on a production model. Two nearly standard Austin-Healeys and a Frazer Nash occupied the next three places, the latter a Le Mans Replica, another over-the-counter racer which could easily be used on the road. Close-to-standard Porsches were competing as were Allards and Aston Martins, and in the following year Triumph TR2s virtually indistinguishable from those in everyday use on the road were raced at Le Mans.

Ten years later, the mid-engined coupé, almost impractical as a road car, had ousted all but a handful of normal, catalogued models. The era of the sports racing car had gone, and the two seat racing car had arrived. So far as international racing was concerned, the traditional sports car was dead, and the chief contestants in what was still called sports car racing were two seat racing cars. The main difference between the 'sports cars' of the 1960s and Can-Am cars, much more honest and straightforward racing tools, lay in matters of detail, like engine size, headlights, and the option of closed or open bodywork.

The Million Dollar Motor Races

The world of the Canadian-American Challenge Cup is a rich one. Ever since the series began in 1966, the prize money has been enormous by any standards–during the years of the Johnson Wax sponsorship, the McLaren team won over a million dollars.

The McLaren domination went back to the early 1960s before the title Can-Am was coined. Instead of taking part in Formula 2 in Europe, to complement his Formula 1 programme Bruce McLaren decided to try sports car racing in America. He used a car called the Zerex Special, which Roger Penske had raced successfully, and did well in American road racing.

The sport at a professional level was still new. Laguna Seca and Riverside were outgrowing their amateur status, and attracting crowds looking for something different: a change from the ovals and dirt tracks that had been traditional in America since racing began.

The road racing revival in the United States after the Second World War began with amateurs who imported European sports cars, and its progress was swift. By the 1960s when the mid-engined car revolution was in full swing, imaginative rules encouraged two-seater racing cars, while Europeans persisted with the term 'sports car'. The Americans swept road car pretences aside, and the cars became racers with full-width bodies. Cooper were established with their Monaco and Lotus with the Type 19, and a new phase in motor racing was ready to begin.

The Zerex had started life as a Cooper Monaco, and as McLaren was still driving for the Cooper Grand Prix team at the time, this was the natural car for him to use, but he replaced the 2.7 litre

CanAm, 1971. Peter Revson, who took the title for McLaren for the fifth time leading Denny Hulme, 1968 and 1970 title winner, in another McLaren-Chevrolet M8F

Above: John Surtees (Lola), winner of the first CanAm series, in 1966
Left: Laguna Seca, 1971. Revson and Hulme lead away at the start of the ninth round in the ten-race series. Their closest challenger was Jackie Stewart with the L & M Lola (left)
Below: Bruce McLaren, winner of the Canadian American Challenge Cup in 1967 and 1969, and a dominating influence on the whole class. He died while testing a new car ten days before the 1970 series was due to start

4 cylinder Coventry-Climax engine with an Oldsmobile V-8.

In the first Can-Am season proper, McLaren could not match John Surtees' Lola powered by the Chevrolet engine, to which McLarens were to turn. Surtees won the first six-race series in 1966 with three wins to one each by Dan Gurney, Mark Donohue, and Phil Hill. Years were to pass before American drivers again figured so prominently, but the series was an immediate success. The awards totalled around $360,000.

The six-race 1967 series was just as rousing, with bigger fields, bigger purses and Ford and Ferrari engines appearing to challenge the dominance of the iron Chevrolet power units. The Lolas were almost eclipsed by the McLaren M6As which won five of the races, leaving the 1966 winners with but a single victory.

Amongst the newcomers to the series were Mike Spence, driving Chris Amon's 1966 McLaren, Roger McCluskey, a veteran of Indianapolis, Ludovico Scarfiotti, and Mario Andretti. Prize money reached a new total of $500,000, of which $210,000 was in guaranteed race purses, and $90,000 in the drivers championship fund, which paid $31,500 for first place, down to $2,700 for tenth. In addition, there was $200,000 for accessory awards, or trade bonuses.

Hulme and McLaren dominated the fields, which included drivers like John Surtees and Dan Gurney, and once again Mark Donohue and Jim Hall. His Chaparral 2F had pioneered a high-mounted aerofoil at the previous year's Bridgehampton race, and in place of its 1966 5.3 litre engine had a 7 litre Chevrolet V-8. These big machines were faster than Formula 1 cars, for example at Mosport, where the Canadian Grand Prix times allowed comparisons. Jim Clark, in a Lotus 49 had earned pole position in the Grand Prix with a 1 minute 22.4 second lap, a speed of 107.9 mph. Hulme's best Can-Am qualifying lap in a McLaren was 1 minute 20.8 seconds, 109.15 mph.

In 1968 the McLarens were no longer giving away a litre to anybody in engine capacity, and were using a new lightweight aluminium Chevrolet engine, and four gears in the Hewland gearbox instead of five. Their M8A was wider, so were the tyres. Denny Hulme won the series, with victories in three races, while Bruce McLaren was second.

Jackie Stewart in the Chaparral 2J. This car 'sucked' itself onto the road by means of fans (lower photograph) which drew out air from beneath the car, and thus increased its road adhesion

The opposition was nonetheless trying harder. Ford was out to break the Chevrolet monopoly, with a four-cam engine which was used in a Lola driven by Mario Andretti, and Peter Revson's non-works McLaren. Yet the Chevrolet held its ground. Ferrari made another attempt to gain a foothold, this time with Chris Amon in a 612 while Pedro Rodriguez raced a P4, but neither were successful. The private entries that made up the bulk of the works McLarens' opposition took comfort from a win by Mark Donohue, and another by London-born Canadian John Cannon, who headed Denny Hulme by over a lap in the rain at Laguna Seca.

Bruce McLaren's own solitary win in 1968 was in the $100,000 Times Grand Prix at Riverside. It seemed to the Americans that McLaren and Hulme were dividing up the series on a value basis. They left only two races as crumbs of comfort to their

A real challenge to McLaren from Porsche developed in 1971. Jo Siffert, here leading Hulme, scored two second places and one third in a Porsche 917 'spyder'

customers, who were lining up to buy new cars for the following season.

In 1969, the opposition seemed keener than ever—Carl Haas was in the field with Simoniz-sponsored cars, and so was Dan Gurney with his 'McLeagle' team; Jim Hall had a series of nasty accidents, which proved a handicap to his Chaparral effort. But the extended eleven race series was won by Bruce McLaren, who took six outright victories to team-mate Hulme's five.

New cars appeared at almost every event, and even if some of the drivers did not reach the professional standards of those at the fronts of the grids, crowds were still rolling up, and enjoying the spectacle of the big, wide racing cars battling it out, or merely pursuing the orange McLarens on some of the finest tracks in the world.

Sadly, the 1969 series was Bruce McLaren's last. While he was testing the 1970 M8D Can-Am car at Goodwood, he crashed and died. Practice for the first race was only ten days away.

McLaren Racing was stunned. For the next two seasons they failed to win a Grand Prix, but still trampled over perhaps the stiffest challenge they had ever faced in Can-Am racing. Neither Porsche nor Ferrari took part officially, but the famous, controversial 'ground effect' Chaparral 2J appeared and because of its speed, especially through corners, threatened the McLarens for the entire series.

On top of everything else, Hulme burned his hands badly in a fire during practice for Indianapolis. McLaren Racing was in some disarray, yet once again the opposition melted away.

The speeds of the 700 horse power monsters were bringing new problems, especially after the FIA's wing ban extended in 1970 to Can-Am. The Sports Car Club of America, which ran the series did not care for the advice that wings made the cars safer by helping to keep them on the ground, when speeds of over 200 mph were becoming commonplace.

Shorn of wings, Jackie Oliver destroyed the promising titanium Autocoast when it flipped on a rise at St Jovite, perhaps due to air turbulence. Also, the wing ban encouraged development of the Chaparral 2J, which 'sucked' itself on to the road like a hovercraft in reverse. Two huge fans driven by an auxiliary engine exhausted air from underneath the car, which in effect then pressed itself down on its tyres with an artificial weight of between 1,800 and 2,500 lbs.

The Chaparral was a sensation. With Jackie Stewart at the wheel, it set new records in the third race of the series at Watkins Glen. It remained a

Denny Hulme cornering hard in the McLaren M8F which he drove to three CanAm victories in 1971

threat in subsequent events, gaining pole position on the starting grids in three out of four races, with Vic Elford at the wheel.

Unfortunately, this arresting technical development was short-lived. Members of the Sports Car Club of America proved as resistant to change in their world as the United States Auto Club had been in theirs (and the CSI in theirs for that matter). Just as USAC virtually banned the turbine car at Indianapolis, so the SCCA capitulated to pressure from teams that the Chaparral had threatened to blow off the tracks, and they banned it too.

Perhaps it would have been different if the Chaparral had not thrown debris 'vacuum-cleaned' from the road at following cars, or not been quite so fast in its first year. It never won any races, because some features proved troublesome, but there can be little doubt that save for the SCCA, the 2J would have been the forerunner of an entirely new concept of racing car. It was a new dimension in the sport.

Of the other new challengers in 1970, George Eaton's BRM proved unreliable, so did the AVS Shadow, and also the March. There were more accidents than usual but Hulme won the series for the second time, backed up by Peter Gethin, who had joined the team following McLaren's death.

In the final Johnson year, 1971, Peter Revson joined the official McLaren team, and this time he won the championship, the first American driver to do so. Jackie Stewart challenged with a Lola, the first time the make had been represented so strongly since that first season in 1966. Yet it was never a match for the 'Orange Elephants', as the McLarens came to be called. The following year, Stewart was to join the McLaren team too.

Interestingly, the 1971 McLaren M8Fs were essentially the same as those that had swept the board in 1968, but their 494 cu (8 litre) Chevrolet V-8s had all-aluminium Reynolds cylinder blocks. These 740 bhp engines proved successful and pointed the way to power units of a capacity exceeding 8 litres.

During the Johnson Wax years, the Can-Am series was a phenomenon, advancing American road racing by a dozen years within the span of half that time. It established in America a new sort of prestigious, well organized motor racing that matched (except, perhaps in the traditions of 70 years) anything in Europe.

The World Wide Scene

A world championship motor race is a major sporting occasion by any standards, attracting a crowd of perhaps a hundred thousand spectators. Each race is only the tip of a pyramid, the brief culmination of the efforts of many people – constructors and component manufacturers, tyre and suspension technologists, spark plug and fuel injection specialists, team mechanics and managers. They have done most of their work before a driver puts on his helmet and lowers himself into the cockpit to drive his car to the grid to play his star role, which in itself is a physically demanding job coming as a climax to hours of test driving and race practice. Then two or three weeks later, the whole process of a race meeting is repeated as the season moves on, from South America and South Africa, through Europe, and on to North America.

No single Grand Prix is typical, or representative of racing as a whole. Tracks are not like rugby pitches or tennis courts, with set dimensions – they are more like golf courses, no two alike in layout, in difficulty, or in character. Just as golf courses have eighteen holes, motor racing tracks have a road, starting and finishing at the same place. Each has a paddock, a sort of parking lot for the racing car transporters, and pits, open-fronted garages with counters facing the track.

A track can be undulating or level. It can be on private ground, or in the more traditional but nowadays less common way it can be on public roads closed for practice and race days. It can have lots of corners, or only a few. How long? Like the proverbial string, as long as it needs to be. Circuits are owned by private individuals, municipalities, companies, or in some cases by clubs. Races are organised by clubs which are in turn sanctioned by a country's principal motor racing club, or more usually in the case of a Grand Prix, by the national club itself, known by the initials ACN (Automobile Club Nationale in motor racing's traditional French).

The responsibilities in motor racing are well-defined. The CSI (Commission Sportive Internationale) makes the rules through a technical sub-committee. It looks after track safety, facilities which constantly have to be brought up to date. Crash barriers, safety fences, and marshals' posts, fire fighting equipment and crash tenders, are permanent features of tracks which bear witness to the fact that motor racing is dangerous. Facilities of this sort are generally better in America than anywhere else.

Given the track, the safety and marshalling installations, and the racing cars, every circuit thereafter takes on its own personality. The Nürburgring twists round the Eifel Mountains, an exciting, exasperating ribbon of road, the longest, most precipitous Grand Prix circuit in the world. Monaco, on the glamorous harbour front is the venue for the race most enthusiasts nominate as the one in the calendar to go and see at the expense of all the others if necessary. Kyalami is on the sun-baked side of a South African hill. At Watkins Glen in the Fall, the Grand Prix circus assembles against the back drop of the vivid colours of upstate New York, for the richest Grand Prix of all. Monza is near smoky Milan, reeks of the drama and history of motor racing, and is the stage for a Grand Prix that invariably provides the most exciting racing of the entire season, as the cars slipstream one another, a few inches apart at nearly 200 miles an hour. At Silverstone the open spaces of the wartime airfield look featureless, but this circuit has the atmosphere of a garden party, a gay amateurism, and a pervading smell not of racing cars, but damp, trodden grass, seemingly inseparable from any English outdoor activity.

Motor racing spectators tend to have an emotional approach to their sport, partly perhaps because of the sense of danger, but also because this activity exemplifies man's control of his machines, and his control of the element of speed not by simply

employing machines, but by his own personal skill. It is the skill of driving—a skill that nearly everyone crowded round the track knows, appreciates, and identifies with every day.

Spectators will camp by the trackside throughout practice, and will remain there for the weekend spectacle of speed, anxious not to miss a moment, or a chance to spot a driver. They want to examine the cars, and write down lap times; they become absorbed with the panoply, the ravishing colour, and the sometimes deafening noise. At Le Mans, huge crowds remain at the race for the entire 24 hours, taking time out perhaps to visit *Le Village* behind the pits, a permanent affair, with restaurants, a fun-fair, exhibitions, and shops, garishly lit, but as integral a part of the Le Mans scene as the pits or the Dunlop Bridge.

The most obvious race officials around a circuit are the flag marshals, who are the main means of communicating with drivers in emergencies. Their blue flags mean another car is close behind. Yellow flags waved mean there is a serious obstruction on the road, perhaps round a corner where there is a crashed car. A yellow and red striped flag warns of an oil patch, a white flag that there is an ambulance or service car on the track, and almost certainly in the way of the racing. A black flag pointed at a driver with his number alongside it, means he must come into the pits at once, and the chequered flag signifies the end of the race. It is only *waved* at the winner.

Races can be ended prematurely by means of a red flag, but this is employed rarely. Even after a serious accident races go on, because this is the tradition in the sport, and also for the very practical reason that it keeps people in their places, and allows the rescue services to get on with their job.

After the 1955 Le Mans disaster, for example, when Pierre Levegh's Mercedes-Benz plunged amongst the spectators with such tragic results, stopping the race would have meant jamming the approach roads with people. Anxious friends would have hampered ambulances, probably exacerbated the panic. When a racing car crashes and the driver is injured, the presence of the race ensures that the track at least will remain clear, and give access of some sort to the accident. The spectators will still watch the race, and no-one gets in anyone else's way.

Opposite, top: Men behind a Grand Prix car, in this case Jackie Stewart's 1970 March 701. Standing, left to right, Dunlop tyre designers and technicians, including Iain Mills and Alec Maskell, Robin Herd, March designer, Keith Duckworth, engine designer, the Tyrrell mechanics, Max Mosley of March, Les Banks of Armstrong, Brian Melia of Autolite, Ray Woods of Lucas, Walter Hayes of Ford and Ken Tyrrell sit on the front wheels. Bottom: a team effort can very quickly come to nothing—Oliver's BRM burns out at Jarama in 1970

The form a race may take is unpredictable, and it can change in a trice. An apparently dull, processional contest can develop suddenly into an exciting close battle when cars in the lead are suddenly eliminated by mechanical failures or accidents. The cars that were trailing them find themselves hoisted into the lead. Their hitherto unimportant dispute becomes instead a duel for one of the biggest prizes in sport, a Grand Prix.

Equally, a promising confrontation between great drivers in great cars can be robbed of interest by a trifle. The great Stewart versus Rindt controversy was never settled, but it might have been in the closing laps of the 1969 British Grand Prix at Silverstone. For sixty laps they had been locked in combat, Stewart in the MS80 Matra, Rindt in the Lotus 49, neither giving an inch, neither making anything on the other. The race had 23 laps to go, and Stewart broke through. But simultaneously Rindt's car's wing fouled a tyre, and the Austrian had to stop. They were never so closely matched again.

The most exciting races of all are those which build up to a climax, or hold their result in doubt till the final moments before the chequered flag. Monza, where the lead can change several times a lap, and the cars race bunched together, has seen some dramatic finishes. Jackie Stewart's Championship win there in 1969 was decided on the last corner, as was his first ever Grand Prix win in 1965 at the same place. John Surtees' 1967 victory with the Honda over Jack Brabham was an equally close-run thing, decided once again in the Parabolica. Peter Gethin's first Grand Prix win in 1971 with the Yardley BRM, was within an ace of being Ronnie Petersen's first Grand Prix win. Or François Cevert's. Or Mike Hailwood's. Or Howden Ganley's. They all finished within a fifth of a second after racing for nearly an hour and a half at 150 mph, and the outcome was decided only in that last corner.

It is not only at Monza that races have been decided so dramatically; in the Silverstone International Trophy in 1962 Graham Hill in the new BRM swept past Jim Clark's Lotus at Woodcote in one of the most daring moves conceivable on this immensely fast bend; at Monaco in 1970 Jack Brabham over-braked into the last corner, and Jochen Rindt swept past to victory.

Yet the palm for one of the most exciting motor races of all time, perhaps because it took a whole 24 hours to build up to a cliff-hanging, nail-biting finish was at Le Mans, in 1969.

The Ford GT40, according to everyone who knew about motor racing, had had its day. The Porsche 908 had won the BOAC 500, Monza 1000 Kms, the Targa Florio, the Spa and Nürburg-

Marshals at work. Left: a flag marshal signalling to an Alfa Romeo
driver that a faster Porsche 917 is overhauling him. Above: quick work
as fuel ignites during a refuelling stop at Brands Hatch; the
silver-suited fire marshal doused the flames with a powder extinguisher
before a blaze took hold

ring 1000 Kms, to set against a lucky Ford win at
Sebring, when the Porsches failed with chassis
trouble. Le Mans was to be the final humiliation of
the GT40 after it had won there for three years in a
row. Porsche had never won the classic French race,
and they had even introduced a new car, the
fabulous 917, to try and win 'The Big One'.

One by one, the Porsches led the race. And one
by one they crashed, or broke down, or slowed,
until there was only one left in the hunt for victory,
the 908 driven by Hans Herrman and Gerard
Larrousse. Incredibly, after being 10 laps behind
the Porsches, by half past ten on the Sunday morning, Jackie Ickx and Jack Oliver had worked their
GT40, a veteran racing car if ever there was one,
into the lead.

Yet the Porsche was still faster. It had proved this
many times. Herrman speeded up, and caught
Ickx. The two cars still had refuelling stops. They
clocked almost identical times at the pits, 44
seconds for one, 45 seconds for the other.

What had been a 24-hour race, over some 3,000
miles at an average speed of just under 130 mph,
was fought out as fast as two drivers could drive in
an hour's close racing to the chequered flag. On the
last lap, the Porsche led down the 200 mph Mulsanne Straight. Near the sharp, right-angled Mulsanne Corner, just before the signalling pits, Ickx
slipstreamed past, and led all the way up the twisty
back leg of the course, through Indianapolis
Corner that used to be surfaced just like 'the Brick-
yard', Arnage, White House, and into the Ford
Chicane to take the cheers and the chequered flag
by a hundred yards. A blink of an eye after a day and
night's motor racing. To Ickx, and Oliver, and
Ford, that Le Mans victory must have been worth
a whole season of lesser races.

Drivers employ tactics of a sort in a race, but
they are rarely detectable in a Grand Prix until
afterwards. There is not much 'lying in wait for the

lead' nowadays. Racing is so competitive that any driver who did this would simply get left behind.

Once upon a time, a driver could play on a rival's suspected lack of stamina, or a deficiency in his brakes, or a weakness in his tyres. There was a famous occasion in the Mille Miglia when Nuvolari drove without his headlights to catch up on his rival Varzi, whose weakness according to Nuvolari was complacency in the lead. But this sort of thing belongs in the romantic age of motor racing. Following another car in the dark along Lake Garda is very different from doing the same thing down the Mulsanne straight at Le Mans.

Driving a modern Grand Prix car is a precision operation. Drivers act as their own on-board computers, sensing things through the seat of their pants and their eyes. The cars are closely matched. Miss a gear and the lead can become third place in an instant, or even fourth. Rival cars often use the same sort of engine, the same tyres and similar transmissions, while monocoque and suspension design has reached the stage where differences in cornering power hardly exist.

Differences in racing cars now lie in matters like the choice of gear ratios. Jackie Stewart puts his win in the 1969 Italian Grand Prix down to the appropriate gear ratio for the last corner of the final lap. He did not need to change gear between the Parabolica and the finishing line. Jochen Rindt did, and he was second.

The fractional advantages are gained by 'tuning' the chassis. Jack Brabham introduced the idea, and soon racing car suspension became adjustable for camber and caster, in spring rates and anti-roll bar resistance, even in the 'give' of the shock absorbers. Tyre pressures can be varied, sometimes the consistency of the tyres themselves. This is the fine adjustment, the Vernier scale of getting the car to its finest pitch of performance before a race. This is what occupies drivers and their team managers in practice. The gear ratios must be right, the car must be set up on its suspension for the corners, geared for the best speed down the straights.

The angle of incidence of the aerofoil 'wing' must be right; steep enough to give downthrust on corners, shallow to absorb least power down the straights. Even braking ratios can be changed to give more stopping power to the front wheels, or more to the back.

The engine nowadays is left untouched. The demon tuners, who could produce an extra 25 horse power by fiercely polishing inside the cylinders or using mysterious valve timing, no longer exist in the higher echelons of racing. There are no magic assemblers, or carburettor wizards nor are there many carburettors left in motor racing. The technologists hold all the secrets. The old empiricism is gone – even the chassis is tuned by the driver.

In touring car racing, or perhaps sometimes in sports car racing, team tactics in the classic pattern can still be seen. Here, a team manager can still reckon that a rival's brakes are suspect, or his transmission always breaks down, or if it rains one car will have an advantage. Here, they can employ the classic gambit of sending the best drivers out with the fastest car to set the pace. They can make the opening hours of a 24 hour event into motor racing of the best sort, not driver racing as in Grands Prix, but motor racing where both man and machine are competing as one, where the teams are made up with more affinity than merely being on the same payroll.

The ploy is to send the fastest driver with the fastest car out on his own. Rivals have no choice but to detach one of *their* cars to keep up. The 'hare' maintains a speed that will not last the entire race, but should he get so far ahead that he can ease off, then he *could* stay the distance. So the opening stages of a race might see all the fastest members of the three-car teams fighting it out at the head of the field, until one by one they blow up, and leave the overnight racing to the less spectacular scorers, with an eye on their tachometers. It is like a cricket match, a war of attrition, and the very essence of the touring or sports car races of the 1920s and 1930s, when to see who would last the course was as important as seeing who would win.

The journalists meanwhile, are writing it all down, or photographing it, or broadcasting it. During the motor racing season, the lead the same sort of nomadic life as the teams. Exotic places like Monaco, Sao Paulo, Johannesburg, or Florida tend to mean the road from the airport, the inside of an hotel, the road to the circuit, and then the same thing all over again in reverse. The hotel-circuit-hotel bit is repeated several times over during the practice days, and after that it is usually back to base to test cars, and write about the latest production figures until the next race.

Public relations men for the teams or the suppliers operate rather like the journalists, but without deadlines to meet, and on more generous budgets. Racing mechanics work hardest of all. Their lot is to get the car prepared, transported and repaired. None of the ease or glamour of jet travel for them, although they are usually on a cut of their car's earnings, which can be considerable.

Worlds apart. Two Porsches in the Targa Florio roar between the ancient houses of a Sicilian street. Below: CanAm cars on the purpose-built Riverside road circuit.

Moments of stress. The strain of clipping the Silverstone corner markers shows in Fangio's face, as he forces his Alfa Romeo 159 on in pursuit of Gonzalez in 1951. Opposite, top: Jack Brabham in his third championship year, 1966, correcting a slide at Zandvoort. Ronnie Peterson locking the right front wheel of his March under fierce braking at Brands Hatch

Often they drive overnight in their transporter, and when they reach the circuit, or the garage where they set up headquarters, preparation of the cars may have to begin at once. Engine changes between practice and the race, and a check-list of items on which their driver's life could depend, means that mechanics tend to see less of life than anyone else. No smart parties or press receptions, certainly not until after the race. Even then, time is short. Cars have to be taken back to the works, stripped down and rebuilt, perhaps repaired again, loaded up and taken to the next race.

The role of tyres in modern racing is a vital one. This technology has reached the point where the compound, the tread, and the construction are critical. Races are often won and lost in the laboratories of Firestone, Goodyear, and Dunlop, the principal makers of racing tyres.

Sponsors, tyre fitters, journalists of both sexes, mechanics, drivers, team managers, public relations men and women, radio reporters, film cameramen, itinerant officials, photographers, ignition specialists, spark plug specialists, designers, spring and damper specialists, lubrication experts, gearbox consultants, wives, girl-friends, mistresses, hangers-on, and even professional spectators, all make up The Circus, that goes racing, especially Grand Prix racing, for eight months of the year.

It is a jealous, exclusive club of professionals. It ignores those not directly involved. Only nomads need apply, and nobody buys their way in. The pretentious rarely remain in for long. Except for some British teams who treat mechanics as Other Ranks it is classless. Nationality and creed simply do not matter; talent and judgment do. A sense of humour is essential, habitual irreverence and an ability to 'fix' things help. Being 'in' is no guarantee of remaining 'in'. You can be 'out' with astonishing swiftness.

The Circus gathers momentum at the early races in South America and South Africa. It travels round Europe in high summer from Silverstone and Brands Hatch and Oulton Park, the Championship and the non-Championship races, to Monaco, Barcelona or Madrid, perhaps Belgium, to one of the French tracks, Germany, Austria, and Italy. There is a Grand Prix every two weeks, and sports car races on the intervening week-ends at Le Mans, or Monza, or Brands Hatch, or Spa, or Nürburgring,

or in Sicily. If there is a week-end spare, there is a Formula 2 race somewhere. Every week-end everybody meets, eats together, drinks together, talks together, occasionally sleeps and sometimes mourns together. On Monday it disintigrates, the fragments flying all over Europe – until the next week-end, and another race.

The first race of the year is like school starting again after the holidays. Monza in September begins the winding-down. It is like the last week of term. Who is driving for whom next season? Who will be writing for whom? Who will be so-and-so's mechanic? Who will be the next champion?

Year in, year out – the round continues in the fascinating, addictive, sensual, exciting World of Motor Racing.

Index

Aerofoils, 38, 123
Alfa Romeo, 13, 40
    P2, 34
    P3, 18, 31, 34
    158/159, 22, 24, 35, 88, 124
    T33, 96, 120, 122
Amercan Grand Prize, 13
    Grand Prix, see United States
        Grand Prix
Amon, C., 67, 114
Andretti, M., 114
Ascari, A., 87, 88
Aston Martin DBR/300, 106
Autocoast, 115
Auto Union, 17, 34

Ballot, 1921 Grand Prix, 32, 33
Bandini, L., 88
Belgian Grand Prix, 13
Bentley, 105
Benz, 1923 Grand Prix, 14
Boillot, G., 12
Bonnier, J., 42, 46
Brabham, J., 39, 42, 48, 67, 73, 79,
    89, 90, 123, 125
Brabham BT20, 49, 68, 89, 125
    BT33, 90
    BT38, 61
Brands Hatch, 29, 95
von Brauchitsch, M., 16
British Grand Prix, 13
BRM, 43
    V-16, 22, 42
    1.5 litre, 43, 51, 81, 91
    2 litre, 87
    2.5 litre, 42
    3 litre, 85
Bugatti, 13
    T30 'Tank', 15
    T35, 15, 34
    T59, 18, 31, 34

Canadian-American Challenge Cup
    (CanAm), 111
Cannon, J., 114
Caracciola, R., 16, 17, 20
Championships, 26, 86
Chapman, C., 35, 38, 44
Chaparral 2F, 108, 114
    2J, 114, 115
Chasseloup-Laubat, G. de, 7
Chevrolet-based CanAm engines,
    114
Chiron, L., 17
Clark, J., 38, 45, 63, 66, 73, 80, 86,
    87, 88, 119

Collins, P. J., 64, 88
Colombo, G., 41
Commission Sportive
    Internationale, 117
Connaught, 26
Cooper, 24
    500 cc, 28, 35
    Cooper-Bristol, 28
    Cooper-Climax, 38, 48, 89
    Monaco, 111
Copp, H., 53
Costin, M., 52
Costs, racing, 58
Cosworth, 52
Crystal Palace, 60
Cunningham sports cars, 108

Daimler, P., 33
Delage V-12, 34
de Dietrich, 9
Drake, D., 56
Duesenberg, 1921 Grand Prix, 14,
    32, 33
Duckworth, K., 52, 118
Duryea, 1895, 8
Dutch Grand Prix, 1968, 76

ERA, 35, 59

Fangio, J. M., 62, 64, 86, 124
Farina, G., 24, 88
Ferrari, Enzo, 34, 40
Ferrari, Scuderia, 18
Ferrari Dino 156, 73, 86
    Dino 246, 50
    P3, 51
    4.5 litre Grand Prix, 24, 25
    312 Grand Prix, 103
    312P, 102
    512, 109
    612, 114
Fiat, 13
    1912 Grand Prix, 11
Fittipaldi, E., 93
Flags, Signal, 119
Flockhart, R., 106
Ford, 49
    GT40, 107, 119
Formulae, 26, 29, 88
    Formula Atlantic, 60
    Formula B, 60
    Formula Junior, 35
    Formula 2, 29, 61
    Formula 3, 35, 61
    Formula Ford, 58
    Formula Vee, 58
French Grand Prix, 1906, 10;
    1912, 12; 1914, 13; 1921, 13
Fuel, 91

Gabriel, F., 8

Gardner, D., 55
German Grand Prix, 13; 1957, 64;
    1968, 77
Gethin, P., 116
Giambertone, M., 65
Ginther, R., 73
Gonzalez, F., 24, 25
Goodwood, 57
Goossen, L., 55
Gordini, 25
Gordon Bennett Races, 10
Goux, J., 12
Grand Prix, first, 10
    Formulae, 26, 29, 88
Gulf-Miller, 21
Gurney, D., 67

Hawthorn, J. M., 28, 50, 64
Hayes, W., 118
Henry, E., 30, 33
Hill, G., 43, 63, 67, 77, 79, 86, 91,
    119
Hill, P., 41, 73, 86
Honda, 3 litre Grand Prix, 67
Hulme, D., 48, 67, 68, 92, 114, 115
HWM,

Ickx, J., 77, 121
Indianapolis 500 Miles Race, 21, 29,
    39
Indianapolis Speedway, 97
Insurance, 58
Ireland, I., 45
Itala, 1913 Grand Prix, 11
Italian Grand Prix, 13, 119;
    1967, 66

Jaguar XK120C, 108
    D-type, 106
Jano, V., 34
Jarama, 118
Jarrott, C., 8, 9
Jenatzy, C., 7
Jenkinson, D., 72
John Player Special, 39, 93

de Knyff, R., 9
Kyalami, 98, 117

Le Mans 24-hour Race, 99, 104, 119
    1955 accident, 26
Levassor, E., 7
Lola T260, 116
Lotus, 44
    12, 45
    18, 38, 46, 72
    25, 38
    49, 38, 63, 66, 68, 69, 80
    33, 63
    56, 37
    72, 39, 45, 93

Macnamara Indianapolis car, 36
McLaren, Bruce, 68, 73, 113
McLaren CanAm cars, 110
    Grand Prix cars, 36, 56, 92
March 701, 118
    713, 85
    721X, 39, 125
Maserati, 1933, 34
    A6GCS, 25
    8CTF, 39
    250F, 65
Matra MS5, 76
    MS10, 77, 78
Mays, R., 43
Mechanics, 123
Mercedes, 1914 Grand Prix, 23, 33
Mercedes-Benz, 17
    W125, 16, 20
    W196, 26, 35, 62
    300SLR, 72
Meyer, L., 56
Mille Miglia, 1955, 72
Miller, H., 55
Miller, rear-engined Indianapolis,
    21
Monaco Grand Prix, 13, 80, 85, 98,
    117; 1961, 72
Monza Autodrome, 17, 98, 99, 119
Mosport, 100
Moss, S., 27, 28, 45, 46, 70, 87, 88,
    106
Murphy, J., 13

Nürburgring, 17, 84, 100, 117
Nuvolari, T., 15, 20

Offenhauser engine, 39, 55

Oliver, J., 115, 121
Ontario Motor Speedway, 101
Osterreichring, 103
Oulton Park, 29, 101.
Owen, Sir A., 44

de Palma, R., 33
Panhard, 7
    1902, 9
Paris-Bordeaux race, 1895, 7
    -Madrid race, 1903, 8
Paul Ricard Circuit, 101
Peterson, R., 61, 125
Peugeot, 1895, 19
    1912 Grand Prix, 12, 30
    1913 Indianapolis, 12
Porsche, Dr. F., 18, 34, 46
Porsche, 46
    911S, 47
    917, 47, 109, 120, 121; CanAm
        variant, 115
    Single-seaters, 47

Renault, L., 8
    1905 Gordon Bennett, 10
Repco-Brabham, 48
Reutemann, C., 61
Revson, P., 114
Rigolly, L., 7
Rindt, J., 45, 83, 86, 88, 100, 119,
    123
Riverside, 122
Rodriguez, P., 62, 114
Rodriguez, R., 62
Rosemeyer, B., 20

Scheckter, J., 61

Shaw, W., 39
Siffert, J., 115
Silverstone, 29, 101, 117
South African Grand Prix, 83
Spa-Francorchamps, 95, 102, 109
Spanish Grand Prix, 82
Speed records, early, 7
Sports car racing, 14, 21, 104
Stewart, J., 29, 50, 51, 54, 61, 74,
    80, 86, 87, 118, 119, 123
Stutz, 105
Surtees, J., 51, 67, 84, 113
Surtees TS7, 84
Swiss Grand Prix, 26

Targa Florio, 17, 96, 122
Tasman Series, 29
Tauranac, R., 48
Town-to-town races, 7
Tracta, 105
von Trips, Count W., 88, 100
Tyrrell, K., 50, 54, 118; Grand
    Prix car, 55
Tyres, 124

Ugolini, N., 64
United States Grand Prix, 83

Vanderbilt Cup, 20
Vanwall, 26, 27, 35
Voiturette racing, 20

Walker, R. R. C., 72, 83
Watkins, Glen, 117

Zerex Special, 111

Acknowledgments

The publishers are grateful to the following for the photographs reproduced in this book:
Associated Press, *Autocar*, Automobile Manufacturers Association, Alice Bixler, Diana Burnett, Eric Dymock, Ford Motor Company, Geoffrey Goddard, Gulf Oil Corporation, Hamlyn Group Library, David Hodges, Keystone, Mercedes-Benz, *Motor*, *Motor Sport*, Shell Photographic Service, Jasper Spencer-Smith, Nigel Snowdon, David Stone, STP, *Sydney Morning Herald*. The paintings on pages 18, 19, 22, 59 and 110 are by Michael Turner.